Mediterranean Bread Machine Cookbook for Beginners

1001-Day Classic and Tasty Recipes for Baking Homemade Bread to help you Lose Weight and Achieve A Healthy Lifestyle

Horls Faltry

© Copyright 2021 Horls Faltry - All Rights Reserved.

In no way is it legal to reproduce, duplicate, or transmit any part of this document by either electronic means or in printed format. Recording of this publication is strictly prohibited, and any storage of this material is not allowed unless with written permission from the publisher. All rights reserved.

The information provided herein is stated to be truthful and consistent, in that any liability, regarding inattention or otherwise, by any usage or abuse of any policies, processes, or directions contained within is the solitary and complete responsibility of the recipient reader. Under no circumstances will any legal liability or blame be held against the publisher for any reparation, damages, or monetary loss due to the information herein, either directly or indirectly.

Respective authors own all copyrights not held by the publisher.

Legal Notice:

This book is copyright protected. This is only for personal use. You cannot amend, distribute, sell, use, quote or paraphrase any part of the content within this book without the consent of the author or copyright owner. Legal action will be pursued if this is breached.

Disclaimer Notice:

Please note the information contained within this document is for educational and entertainment purposes only. Every attempt has been made to provide accurate, up-to-date and reliable, complete information. No warranties of any kind are expressed or implied. Readers acknowledge that the author is not engaging in the rendering of legal, financial, medical or professional advice.

By reading this document, the reader agrees that under no circumstances are we responsible for any losses, direct or indirect, which are incurred as a result of the use of information contained within this document, including, but not limited to, errors, omissions, or inaccuracies.

Table of Contents

Introduction 5
Chapter 1: Basics of Mediterranean Diet 6
    What Is the Mediterranean Diet? 6
    The History of The Mediterranean Diet 6
    Benefits of The Mediterranean Diet 7
Chapter 2: Basics of Bread Machine 9
    Control Panel of Bread Machine 9
    Bread Maker Program Cycles 11
    Benefits of Using Bread Make 12
    Cleaning and Maintenance 13
Chapter 3: Basic Bread 14
    Whole Wheat Maple Bread 14
    Pumpkin Bread 15
    Basic White Bread 16
    Easy English Muffin Bread 17
    Cornbread Loaf 18
    Semolina Bread 19
    Sandwich Bread 20
    Basic Whole Wheat Bread 21
    Oatmeal Bread 22
    Honey Milk Bread 23
    Buttermilk Honey Bread 24
    Cocoa Bread 25
    Simple Country White Bread 26
    Quick White Bread 27
    French Bread Loaf 28
    Multigrain Bread 29
Chapter 4: Fruit & Vegetable Bread 30
    Onion Bread Loaf 30
    Olive Bread Loaf 31
    Raisin Apple Bread 32
    Greek Tomato Basil Bread 33
    Flavorful Apricot Bread Loaf 34
    Raisin Cinnamon Bread 35
    Blueberry Bread Loaf 36
    Rosemary Olive Bread 37
    Feta Olives Bread 38
    Walnut Blueberry Bread Loaf 39
    Zucchini Bread 40
    Pumpkin Walnut Bread 41
    Mushroom Bread 42
    Italian Pesto Bread 43
    Sweet Potato Bread 44
    Banana Walnut Bread 45
Chapter 5: Spice & Herb Bread 46
    Delicious Garlic Bread 46
    Caraway Bread 47
    Delicious Herb Bread 48
    Rosemary Thyme Bread 49
    Rosemary Sun-Dried Tomato Bread .. 50
    Rosemary Thyme Orange Bread 51
    Cinnamon Bread 52
    Herb French Bread 53
    Flavors Herb Bread 54
    Tomato Rosemary Bread 55
    Herb Zucchini Bread 56
    Greek Herb Bread 57

Dill Pepper Bread 58	Cajun Bread 60
Jalapeno Bread 59	Tasty Dill Pickle Bread 61

Chapter 6: Cheese Bread 62

Pepperoni Cheese Bread 62	Basil Oregano Thyme Cheese Bread .. 70
Basil Garlic Parmesan Bread 63	Easy Cheesy Bread Loaf 71
Easy Cheese Jalapeno Bread 64	Cranberry Cream Cheese Bread 72
Pepper Jack Cheese Bread 65	Cream Cheese Bread 73
Healthy Cheese Bread 66	Cheese Beer Bread 74
Buttermilk Cheese Bread 67	Asiago Cheese Bread 75
Italian Cheddar Cheese Bread 68	Parmesan Herb Bread 76
Cheddar Cheese Bread 69	Easy Cheddar Bread 77

Chapter 7: Sweet Bread 78

Portuguese Bread 78	Chocolate Chip Bread 86
Nut Banana Bread Loaf 79	Choco Chip Pumpkin Bread 87
Cinnamon Apple Bread 80	Chocolate Bread 88
Cranberry Cinnamon Bread 81	Coffee Bread 89
Sweet Honey Whole Wheat Bread 82	Pumpkin Spice Bread 90
Buttermilk Apple Bread 83	Cardamom Cranberry Bread 91
Delicious Pumpkin Bread 84	Honey Oatmeal Sunflower Bread 92
Cranberry Bread 85	Sweet Maple Bread 93

Chapter 8: Gluten-Free Bread 94

Moist Sandwich Bread 94	Gluten-Free Bread 101
Coconut Flour Bread 95	Gluten-Free Banana Bread 102
Whole-Grain Bread 96	Gluten-Free French Bread 103
Gluten-Free Flour Bread 97	Multiseed Multigrain Sandwich Bread 104
Sandwich Bread 98	
Gluten-Free Cinnamon Raisin Bread 99	

Chapter 9: Sourdough Bread 105

Healthy Sourdough Bread 105	Simple Sourdough Bread 110
Jalapeno Cheddar Sourdough Bread 106	Basic Sourdough Bread 111
Sourdough Rye Bread 107	Maple Oat Sourdough Bread 112
Soft Whole Wheat Sourdough Bread 108	Gluten-Free Bread 113
	Easy Sourdough Bread 114
Whole Wheat Sandwich Bread 109	

Conclusion 115

Introduction

Would you like to make mouth-watering home-made Mediterranean bread? Do you want to learn the secrete recipes of expert Mediterranean bakers? If your answer is Yes, this book is for you. It is going to be your favorite Mediterranean Bread Machine Cookbook!

Mediterranean Bread Machine Cookbook for Beginners contains the basic principles of the Mediterranean bread. Including 1001-Day classic and tasty recipes for baking homemade bread to help you lose weight and achieve a healthy lifestyle.

In order to finally achieve your weight loss goals and optimum health you need to be following a plan that is sustainable long term. Let's go on this cookbook and look for the Mediterranean bread that will allow us to eliminate that stubborn body fat.

Chapter 1: Basics of Mediterranean Diet

What Is the Mediterranean Diet?

When studied historically the Mediterranean diet can be tied to a specific region or era. But scientifically proven the Mediterranean diet taken a much universally place in human history. Due to its unique approach to food consumption, it brings more balance to our diet and fills our plate with a healthy nutritional meal in a proportionate amount. It is an innate human need to consume food of all sorts, ranging from protein-rich meats to the fiber loaded vegetables, and fruits and the carb filled grains. So, this diet only works in light of such need. Its emphasis more on clean fats and healthy oils for daily consumption. The diet carried its name from its origin, which is rooted in the region around the Mediterranean Sea. People from those places were more reliant on seafood, fresh vegetables, fruits, olive oil, and whole grains. Their approach rightly guided the world to a nutrient-rich meal plan.

The greatest thing about the Mediterranean diet is it does not only guarantee good health, but it comes with so much flavor, aroma, and colors for our platters. Unlike, other restrictive diets, the Mediterranean diet is much more open and flexible. It suggests so many delectable options for every taste palate that it is easy for anyone to adopt. Over the course of time, the Mediterranean diet has significantly evolved according to different regions and culinary cultures. Today, it manages to prevent and cure several life-threatening diseases.

The History of The Mediterranean Diet

The Mediterranean diet that exists today originated from the stretches of Greece and Italy. Different classes of those societies individually contributed to the formation of this diet. There was a great inclination towards the eating of white omega rich meat including all seafood. Along with that, they use to consume lots of vegetables, fruits, and grains in some amount. The typical food patterns of the people in those areas were adopted readily by many due to the diversity of the nutrients the Mediterranean pyramid has provided. Over the years it existed as a culinary tradition, it was not until 1975 when American biologist Ansel keys and Margaret key collaborated to publicize the Mediterranean diet as a health-oriented meal plan. However, its widespread recognition came late in the 1990s. Studies regarding the benefits of this diet were conducted in Madrid and Naples; the objective data obtained revealed significant results. This study confirms the wide-ranging effects of the

Mediterranean diet over people's health which were predicted decades ago. Later scientists came up with their different versions of the Mediterranean diet, but the one which was readily adopted was given by Walter Willet and his colleagues in mid-1990s. This approach was closest to the naturally evolved Mediterranean diet. It suggests a similar pattern of food intake as the people from ancient Greece did.

Benefits of The Mediterranean Diet

A healthy diet can do miracles no medicine can guarantee. Mediterranean diet is no less than miraculous if we acknowledge the great benefits it brings to human health. Besides accelerating the rate of metabolism and detoxifying the body from harmful oxidants, this diet can deal with a range of mental and physical ailments including cancer, cardiovascular disorders, and Parkinson, etc.

1. **Prevent Alzheimer and Parkinson:**
   Both Parkinson and Alzheimer are neural disorders which result from the toxic build up in the brain and damage caused by it. The Mediterranean diet has shown unbelievable effects over the patients of Parkinson and Alzheimer, and they all experience improved mental functioning because of this diet plan.

2. **Fights Against Cardiovascular Diseases:**
   All the cardiovascular diseases are linked with high blood cholesterol levels or weakening of the cardiac muscles. With the Mediterranean diet, such threats can be fought due to its good fat content. It does not allow the accumulation of bad fats and toxins in the body while keeping the metabolism active and running all the time.

3. **Lowers Bad Cholesterol:**
   The olive oil based Mediterranean diet is free from all the saturated fats. Resultantly it is low on bad cholesterol. This form of cholesterol is responsible for blocking the blood vessels and causes a high blood cholesterol level.

4. **High Life Expectancies:**
   Good diet and longevity have a very real connection. The better you eat, the healthier you stay. When you eat everything and balance, it can guarantee a long life. This fact is happened to be true for people consuming a Mediterranean diet, and therefore it is prescribed to everyone looking for higher life expectancy.

5. **Aids Cancer Treatment:**
Another curse of the current age is incurable cancer and the like diseases. Where most of the medicinal and chemical therapies fail to cure the disease, a change in diet have proven miraculous for most of the cancer patients. Mediterranean diet has been proven the most beneficial in this regard. People who are already consuming this diet shows about a sixty percent lesser tendency of developing cancer than the people who don't consume it.

Chapter 2: Basics of Bread Machine

Control Panel of Bread Machine

The bread machine comes with a digital display screen and six buttons to make your bread-making process faster and easy. The digital display panel will help to know the remaining time of the program cycle and also help to set the desire hardness settings of the crust.

- **Programmed Cycles**

The program cycle is chosen or identified by their number. Following are the list of program cycle printed on the top of the bread maker lid.

1. Basic
2. French
3. Gluten-Free
4. Quick
5. Sweet
6. 1.5 lb Express
7. 2.0 lb Express
8. Dough
9. Jam
10. Cake
11. Whole Grain
12. Bake

- **CYCLE Button**

Press the cycle button again and again until you have selected the desire cooking cycle program. The cycle number is shown on the display panel.

- **CRUST Colour Button**

Using this button you can select the desire crust color from light, medium, and dark options. If you want to make a soft and light crust then you have to select the light option. If you want darker and crispier crust then select the dark option.

Press the Crust button and move the arrow on Light, Medium, and Dark settings to select the desire crust settings. You cannot allow adjusting the crust settings if you are using 8 (Dough), 9 (Jam), 10 (Cake), 11 (Whole Grain), and 12 (Bake) programmed cycles.

- **LOAF SIZE Button**

Using this button you can select the loaf size from 1.5 lb or 2.0 lb options.

Press the Loaf size button until the arrow pointer set either 1.5lb or 2.0 lb. The loaf size is not options in 4 (Quick), 6 (1.5 lb Express), 7 (2.0 lb Express), 8 (Dough), 9 (Jam), 10 (Cake) and 12 (Bake) programmed cycle.

- **DELAY TIMER Buttons**

This Function is one of the favorite functions of those people who live a busy lifestyle. Using this function you can plan your meal ahead of time. You just need to add all the ingredients into the bread maker machine and set the delay time. The fresh and hot breakfast is ready to serve as per your set time.

Use the + or − button to increase or decrease the delay program cycle time shown on display. You can only set the delay time after selecting the program cycle, crust color, and loaf size. The 6(1.5 lb Express), 7 (2.0 lb Express) and 9 (Jam) cycle doesn't use delay function.

- **START/STOP Button**

Using this button you can start or stop the cycle at any time.

Press the START/STOP button once will start the cycle. When you heard a short beep it means that the cycle is started. After finishing the cycle press START/STOP again to end the cycle and remove your fresh bread. If you want to cancel the cycle during the baking process then press the START/STOP button for 2 seconds.

- **KEEP WARM**

After finishing the baking cycle the machine will automatically shift to Keep Warm settings and this process will run for 1 hour.

If you want to cancel the keep warm settings then press the START/STOP button for 2 seconds. It will shut down the machine completely.

- **POWER FAILURE**

During the baking process if any power interruption, the baking process continues only if the power is back within 5 minutes. If the power failure is more than 5 minutes then the machine will cancel the current setting and revert to default settings. The default settings are programmed cycle 1 (Basic), crust medium and loaf size is 2.0 lb Express. If the dough is not into the rising phase then you can start the program cycle again from the beginning.

- **DISPLAY WARNING**

The digital display blinks and gives warning messages like HHH or LLL. Where the "HHH" warning message indicates that the inside temperature of the bread pan goes high. In this situation stop the current working program and unplug the power cord. Open the machine cover and let it cool down before restarting the program cycle. Where the "LLL" message indicates that the inside temperature of the bread pan goes very low for the bread-making process.

Bread Maker Program Cycles

The Bread maker offers 12 program cycles.

1. **Basic:** The basic cycle is used for all-purpose simple recipes especially white bread. It is ideal settings for basic bread flour recipes.
2. **French:** These settings are not just for making French bread you can also bake European style bead using these settings. The French bread settings give a nice crusty exterior and soft inside texture to your bread.
3. **Gluten-Free:** The Hamilton bead makes offers a special cycle for baking gluten-free bread. If you are on any special diet then gluten-free bread is a healthy choice for you. These settings are ideal for gluten-free bread and mixes.
4. **Quick:** This cycle is ideal for quick bread recipes where the recipes are done without adding yeast. The recipes did under this cycle these recipes don't require rising time and can be baked immediately.
5. **Sweet:** These cycles especially design to make sweet yeast bread. The bread with additives like dry fruits, added sugar, raisins, fruit juices, and more. This cycle takes a longer phase for the rising dough to make your bread light and airy.
6. **1.5 lb Express:** These settings are specially designed for making loaf under 2 hours. This cycle is used for a smaller loaf. Using quick-rising yeast occurs the loaf within 58 minutes.
7. **2.0 lb Express:** This cycle is ideal for large size loaf otherwise it works the same as the 1.5 lb express cycle.
8. **Dough:** This cycle is ideal for making dough for rolls, pizza, pie crust, coffee cake, cookie dough, and many types of dough that you want to bake into your oven. This cycle has no baking functionality.

9. **Jam:** Using this cycle you can make homemade fresh fruit jams. To get the best results cut your fruits into cubes before starting the jam-making cycle. During jam making process the internal temperature of the machine is a little high and the kneading blade paddle stirs the jam continuously.
10. **Cake:** This cycle is ideal for the baking cake into your bread maker machine.
11. **Whole Grain:** Whole wheat or rye flour is used in the whole grain cycle. This cycle takes longer kneading, rising time, and preheats time to expand the heavy grains.
12. **Bake:** This cycle is used to bake the dough. If you use the bake cycle for a longer period of time then you will get a nice dark crust over the loaf.

Benefits of Using Bread Make

The bread maker machine comes with various types of benefits some of the important benefits are given as follows.

- **Easy to use**

The bread machines are easy to use comes with a display panel and a few buttons anyone can easily operate the machine by just selecting the proper program cycle. You just need to add the precise amount of ingredients into the bread maker and select the functions given in the recipe and done. Your bread machine will bake fresh, soft, and tasty bread.

- **Multi-tasking features**

Today's bread-making machines are designed for multi-tasking purposes so you not only bake the different kinds of bread into your bead make but also used to make jam, pizza dough, cakes, cookie dough, and many more. When you want to bake different varieties of food for birthday parties and festival seasons the bread makes helps you to prepare these foods without making a mess.

- **Saves Money**

As we know that the oven requires a high amount of electricity than other home appliances. The bread maker machine is energy-efficient appliances require very less electricity to perform their operations. It also reduces raw material costing by reducing wastage. In some cases, if you didn't knead the dough properly or add a little amount of yeast into the dough then your dough not rising properly. Bread maker doing all these processes automatically with perfection after adding the right amount of ingredients.

- **Control over Ingredients**

Using a beading machine you can make healthy and fresh bread at your home. If you are following any diet then you have to prefer to make gluten-free, whole-grain bread and add them to your diet. While making bread you can also use healthy ingredients like dry fruits, herbs, fruits, cheese, vegetables, sundried tomatoes, and more.

Cleaning and Maintenance

1. Before starting the cleaning process first unplug the appliance and let it cool down at room temperature.
2. Remove the kneading paddle for cleaning. If it is difficult to remove then add water into the bottom of the bread pan and soak it for up to 1 hour. The kneading paddle is dishwasher safe you can also clean it with a damp cloth.
3. Remove the bread pan from the bread maker by just turning it in a clockwise direction. The bread pan comes with a non-stick coating so do not use abrasive cleaning agents to protect the coatings. You can simply wipe the bread pan from inside and outside with a damp cloth.
4. Clean the housing and lid, baking chamber, and viewing window with the help of a damp cloth. Do not immerse the housing in water it may damage your appliance.
5. After drying all the parts thoroughly place them into its original position. Now your bread maker is ready for next use.

Chapter 3: Basic Bread

Whole Wheat Maple Bread

Preparation Time: 10 minutes
Cooking Time: 2 hours 53 minutes
Serve: 12

Ingredients:

- 2 cups bread flour
- 1 1/2 tsp bread machine yeast
- 1 cup whole wheat flour
- 2 tbsp butter, melted
- 2 tbsp maple syrup
- 2 tbsp dry milk
- 1 cup buttermilk
- 1 tsp salt

Directions:

1. Add all ingredients to the breadmaker pan.
2. Select the basic bread cycle then select loaf size 1.5 pound and select crust color medium. Press start.
3. Once done, remove the bread loaf from the breadmaker.
4. Let cool bread loaf for 10 minutes.
5. Slice and serve.

Nutritional Value (Amount per Serving):

- Calories 150
- Fat 2.5 g
- Carbohydrates 27.4 g
- Sugar 3.2 g
- Protein 4.2 g
- Cholesterol 6 mg

Pumpkin Bread

Preparation Time: 10 minutes
Cooking Time: 2 hours 53 minutes
Serve: 12

Ingredients:

- 4 cups bread flour
- 2 1/4 tsp active dry yeast
- 2 tbsp sugar
- 1 cup can pumpkin puree
- 1/2 cup milk
- 2 tbsp olive oil
- 1 1/4 tsp salt

Directions:

1. Add all ingredients to the bread maker pan.
2. Select the basic bread cycle then select loaf size 1.5 pound and select crust color light. Press start.
3. Once done, remove the bread loaf from the bread maker.
4. Let cool bread loaf for 10 minutes.
5. Slice and serve.

Nutritional Value (Amount per Serving):

- Calories 190
- Fat 3 g
- Carbohydrates 35.4 g
- Sugar 2.9 g
- Protein 5 g
- Cholesterol 1 mg

Basic White Bread

Preparation Time: 10 minutes
Cooking Time: 2 hours 53 minutes
Serve: 12

Ingredients:

- 3 cups white flour
- 1 1/2 tbsp dry milk powder
- 1 1/2 tsp bread machine yeast
- 2 tbsp sugar
- 2 tbsp butter
- 1 1/4 cups water
- 1 1/2 tsp salt

Directions:

1. Add water, sugar, butter, salt, dry milk powder, flour, and bread machine yeast in the bread maker pan.
2. Select the basic bread cycle then select loaf size 1.5 pound and select crust color medium. Press start.
3. Once done, remove the bread loaf from the bread maker.
4. Let cool bread loaf for 10 minutes.
5. Slice and serve.

Nutritional Value (Amount per Serving):

- Calories 143
- Fat 2.3 g
- Carbohydrates 26.6 g
- Sugar 2.6 g
- Protein 3.8 g
- Cholesterol 5 mg

Easy English Muffin Bread

Preparation Time: 10 minutes
Cooking Time: 2 hours 53 minutes
Serve: 12

Ingredients:

- 3 1/2 cups all-purpose flour
- 2 1/4 tsp instant yeast
- 1/2 tsp baking powder
- 1 1/2 tsp sugar
- 2 tbsp vegetable oil
- 1 cup lukewarm milk
- 1/4 cup water
- 1 tsp vinegar
- 1 1/2 tsp salt

Directions:

1. Add all ingredients to the bread maker pan.
2. Select the basic bread cycle then select loaf size 1.5 pound and select crust color light. Press start.
3. Once done, remove the bread loaf from the bread maker.
4. Let cool bread loaf for 10 minutes.
5. Slice and serve.

Nutritional Value (Amount per Serving):

- Calories 167
- Fat 3.1 g
- Carbohydrates 29.7 g
- Sugar 1.5 g
- Protein 4.7 g
- Cholesterol 2 mg

Cornbread Loaf

Preparation Time: 10 minutes
Cooking Time: 1 hour 40 minutes
Serve: 12

Ingredients:

- 2 eggs, lightly beaten
- 17 oz corn muffin mix
- 1/2 tsp bread machine yeast
- 1 cup milk

Directions:

1. Add all ingredients to the breadmaker pan.
2. Select the quick bread cycle then select crust color light. Press start.
3. Once done, remove the bread loaf from the breadmaker.
4. Let cool bread loaf for 10 minutes.
5. Slice and serve.

Nutritional Value (Amount per Serving):

- Calories 172
- Fat 5.7 g
- Carbohydrates 28.2 g
- Sugar 8 g
- Protein 3.7 g
- Cholesterol 34 mg

Semolina Bread

Preparation Time: 10 minutes
Cooking Time: 3 hours
Serve: 16

Ingredients:

- 2 1/4 cups semolina flour
- 2 cups bread flour
- 2 tsp dry yeast
- 2 tsp sea salt
- 1/4 cup barley malt syrup
- 6 tbsp olive oil
- 1 1/2 cups warm water

Directions:

1. Add all ingredients to the bread maker pan.
2. Select the basic bread cycle then select loaf size 2 pound and select crust color light. Press start.
3. Once done, remove the bread loaf from the bread maker.
4. Let cool bread loaf for 10 minutes.
5. Slice and serve.

Nutritional Value (Amount per Serving):

- Calories 203
- Fat 5.7 g
- Carbohydrates 32.7 g
- Sugar 2 g
- Protein 5 g
- Cholesterol 0 mg

Sandwich Bread

Preparation Time: 10 minutes
Cooking Time: 2 hours 53 minutes
Serve: 12

Ingredients:

- 3 cups bread flour
- 1/4 cup olive oil
- 2 1/4 tsp bread machine yeast
- 2 tbsp sugar
- 1 cup of warm water
- 1 1/4 tsp salt

Directions:

1. Add all ingredients to the breadmaker pan.
2. Select the basic bread cycle then select loaf size 1.5 pound and select crust color medium. Press start.
3. Once done, remove the bread loaf from the breadmaker.
4. Let cool bread loaf for 10 minutes.
5. Slice and serve.

Nutritional Value (Amount per Serving):

- Calories 159
- Fat 4.5 g
- Carbohydrates 26.1 g
- Sugar 2.1 g
- Protein 3.5 g
- Cholesterol 0 mg

Basic Whole Wheat Bread

Preparation Time: 10 minutes
Cooking Time: 2 hours 53 minutes
Serve: 12

Ingredients:

- 3 cups whole wheat flour
- 2 tsp dry yeast
- 1 1/2 tbsp sugar
- 1 1/8 cups water
- 1 1/2 tsp salt

Directions:

1. Add all ingredients to the bread maker pan.
2. Select the whole grain bread cycle then select loaf size 1.5 pound. Press start.
3. Once done, remove the bread loaf from the bread maker.
4. Let cool bread loaf for 10 minutes.
5. Slice and serve.

Nutritional Value (Amount per Serving):

- Calories 121
- Fat 0.3 g
- Carbohydrates 25.6 g
- Sugar 1.6 g
- Protein 3.5 g
- Cholesterol 0 mg

Oatmeal Bread

Preparation Time: 10 minutes
Cooking Time: 2 hours 53 minutes
Serve: 12

Ingredients:

- 3 cups bread flour
- 2 tsp yeast
- 1 egg, lightly beaten
- 1/2 cup oats
- 1 tbsp molasses
- 3 tbsp honey
- 2 tbsp butter
- 1 cup boiling water
- 1 1/2 tsp salt

Directions:

1. Add oats and boiling water to the bowl and set aside.
2. Once oats are cooled then add into the breadmaker pan.
3. Add remaining ingredients to the breadmaker pan.
4. Select the basic bread cycle then select loaf size 1.5 pound and select crust color light. Press start.
5. Once done, remove the bread loaf from the breadmaker.
6. Let cool bread loaf for 10 minutes.
7. Slice and serve.

Nutritional Value (Amount per Serving):

- Calories 172
- Fat 2.8 g
- Carbohydrates 32 g
- Sugar 5.4 g
- Protein 4.4 g
- Cholesterol 19 mg

Honey Milk Bread

Preparation Time: 10 minutes
Cooking Time: 2 hours 53 minutes
Serve: 12

Ingredients:

- 3 cups bread flour
- 2 tsp active dry yeast
- 3 tbsp butter, melted
- 3 tbsp honey
- 1 cup milk
- 1 1/2 tsp salt

Directions:

1. Add all ingredients to the bread maker pan.
2. Select the basic bread cycle then select loaf size 1.5 pound and select crust color medium. Press start.
3. Once done, remove the bread loaf from the bread maker.
4. Let cool bread loaf for 10 minutes.
5. Slice and serve.

Nutritional Value (Amount per Serving):

- Calories 167
- Fat 3.6 g
- Carbohydrates 29.4 g
- Sugar 5.3 g
- Protein 4.2 g
- Cholesterol 9 mg

Buttermilk Honey Bread

Preparation Time: 10 minutes
Cooking Time: 2 hours 53 minutes
Serve: 12

Ingredients:

- 3 cups bread flour
- 1/2 cup water
- 3 tbsp honey
- 3 tsp butter, softened
- 3/4 cup buttermilk
- 2 tsp yeast
- 1 1/2 tsp salt

Directions:

1. Add all ingredients to the bread maker pan.
2. Select the basic bread cycle then select loaf size 1.5 pound and select crust color medium. Press start.
3. Once done, remove the bread loaf from the bread maker.
4. Let cool bread loaf for 10 minutes.
5. Slice and serve.

Nutritional Value (Amount per Serving):

- Calories 146
- Fat 1.4 g
- Carbohydrates 29.2 g
- Sugar 5.1 g
- Protein 4 g
- Cholesterol 3 mg

Cocoa Bread

Preparation Time: 10 minutes
Cooking Time: 2 hours 53 minutes
Serve: 12

Ingredients:

- 1 egg
- 1 egg yolk
- 1 cup milk
- 3 cups bread flour
- 2 1/2 tsp bread machine yeast
- 1 tbsp vital wheat gluten
- 1/3 cup cocoa powder
- 1/2 cup brown sugar
- 1 tsp vanilla
- 3 tbsp canola oil
- 1 tsp salt

Directions:

1. Add all ingredients to the breadmaker pan.
2. Select the basic bread cycle then select loaf size 1.5 pound and select crust color medium. Press start.
3. Once done, remove the bread loaf from the breadmaker.
4. Let cool bread loaf for 10 minutes.
5. Slice and serve.

Nutritional Value (Amount per Serving):

- Calories 206
- Fat 5.4 g
- Carbohydrates 33 g
- Sugar 7 g
- Protein 7.3 g
- Cholesterol 33 mg

Simple Country White Bread

Preparation Time: 10 minutes
Cooking Time: 2 hours 53 minutes
Serve: 12

Ingredients:

- 2 1/2 cups all-purpose flour
- 1 1/2 tsp sugar
- 1 tbsp olive oil
- 2 1/2 tsp bread machine yeast
- 1/4 tsp baking soda
- 1 cup bread flour
- 1 1/2 cups lukewarm water
- 1 tsp salt

Directions:

1. Add all ingredients to the bread maker pan.
2. Select the basic bread cycle then select loaf size 1.5 pound and select crust color medium. Press start.
3. Once done, remove the bread loaf from the bread maker.
4. Let cool bread loaf for 10 minutes.
5. Slice and serve.

Nutritional Value (Amount per Serving):

- Calories 147
- Fat 1.6 g
- Carbohydrates 28.6 g
- Sugar 0.6 g
- Protein 4.1 g
- Cholesterol 0 mg

Quick White Bread

Preparation Time: 10 minutes
Cooking Time: 58 minutes
Serve: 12

Ingredients:

- 3 1/4 cups bread flour
- 1 tbsp instant yeast
- 2 tbsp dry milk
- 2 tbsp butter, melted
- 3 tbsp sugar
- 1 cup of warm water
- 1/2 tsp salt

Directions:

1. Add all ingredients to the breadmaker pan.
2. Select the express bread cycle then select crust color dark. Press start.
3. Once done, remove the bread loaf from the breadmaker.
4. Let cool bread loaf for 10 minutes.
5. Slice and serve.

Nutritional Value (Amount per Serving):

- Calories 156
- Fat 2.4 g
- Carbohydrates 29.3 g
- Sugar 3.2 g
- Protein 4 g
- Cholesterol 5 mg

French Bread Loaf

Preparation Time: 10 minutes
Cooking Time: 3 hours 40 minutes
Serve: 12

Ingredients:

- 3 1/2 cups bread flour
- 1 1/2 tsp bread machine yeast
- 1 tsp sugar
- 1 cup of water
- 1 tsp salt

Directions:

1. Add all ingredients to the breadmaker pan.
2. Select the french bread cycle then select loaf size 1.5 pound and select crust color dark. Press start.
3. Once done, remove the bread loaf from the breadmaker.
4. Let cool bread loaf for 10 minutes.
5. Slice and serve.

Nutritional Value (Amount per Serving):

- Calories 135
- Fat 0.4 g
- Carbohydrates 28.3 g
- Sugar 0.4 g
- Protein 4 g
- Cholesterol 0 mg

Multigrain Bread

Preparation Time: 10 minutes
Cooking Time: 2 hours 53 minutes
Serve: 12

Ingredients:

- 1 1/2 cups bread flour
- 2 1/2 tsp bread machine yeast
- 3 tbsp brown sugar
- 1 cup multigrain cereal
- 1 1/2 cups whole wheat flour
- 2 tbsp butter, softened
- 1 1/2 cups water
- 1 1/4 tsp salt

Directions:

1. Add all ingredients to the breadmaker pan.
2. Select the basic bread cycle then select loaf size 1.5 pound and select crust color medium. Press start.
3. Once done, remove the bread loaf from the breadmaker.
4. Let cool bread loaf for 10 minutes.
5. Slice and serve.

Nutritional Value (Amount per Serving):

- Calories 153
- Fat 2.4 g
- Carbohydrates 28.5 g
- Sugar 2.4 g
- Protein 4 g
- Cholesterol 5 mg

Chapter 4: Fruit & Vegetable Bread

Onion Bread Loaf

Preparation Time: 10 minutes
Cooking Time: 2 hours 53 minutes
Serve: 12

Ingredients:

- 3 1/2 cup bread flour
- 2 tbsp dried onion, minced
- 2 tsp bread machine yeast
- 2 tbsp olive oil
- 1 tbsp sugar
- 1 cup of water
- 1 1/8 tsp salt

Directions:

1. Add all ingredients to the bread maker pan.
2. Select the basic bread cycle then select loaf size 1.5 pound and select crust color medium. Press start.
3. Once done, remove the bread loaf from the bread maker.
4. Let cool bread loaf for 10 minutes.
5. Slice and serve.

Nutritional Value (Amount per Serving):

- Calories 58
- Fat 2.4 g
- Carbohydrates 7.8 g
- Sugar 1.4 g
- Protein 1.5 g
- Cholesterol 0 mg

Olive Bread Loaf

Preparation Time: 10 minutes
Cooking Time: 2 hours 53 minutes
Serve: 12

Ingredients:

- 1 2/3 cups whole wheat flour
- 1/2 cup olives, pitted & chopped
- 2 tsp active dry yeast
- 1 1/2 tsp dried basil
- 2 tbsp sugar
- 3 cups bread flour
- 2 tbsp olive oil
- 1 cup of warm water
- 1/3 cup brine from olives
- 1 1/2 tsp salt

Directions:

1. Add all ingredients except olives to the bread maker pan.
2. Select the basic bread cycle then select loaf size 1.5 pound and select crust color medium. Press start.
3. Add olives once add ingredient signal beeps.
4. Once done, remove the bread loaf from the bread maker.
5. Let cool bread loaf for 10 minutes.
6. Slice and serve.

Nutritional Value (Amount per Serving):

- Calories 214
- Fat 3.5 g
- Carbohydrates 39.8 g
- Sugar 2.1 g
- Protein 5.3 g
- Cholesterol 0 mg

Raisin Apple Bread

Preparation Time: 10 minutes
Cooking Time: 58 minutes
Serve: 8

Ingredients:

- 2 eggs, lightly beaten
- 1 tsp vanilla
- 1 tsp cinnamon
- 5 1/2 tbsp sugar
- 5 1/2 tbsp butter, melted
- 3 tsp baking powder
- 1 1/2 cups all-purpose flour
- 1/4 cup milk
- 1/4 cup walnuts, chopped
- 1/4 cup raisins
- 1 small apple, peel & chopped

Directions:

1. Add all ingredients except raisins, walnut, and apple to the bread maker pan.
2. Select the express bread cycle then select crust color medium. Press start.
3. Add raisins, walnut, and apple once add ingredient signal beeps.
4. Once done, remove the bread loaf from the bread maker.
5. Let cool bread loaf for 10 minutes.
6. Slice and serve.

Nutritional Value (Amount per Serving):

- Calories 262
- Fat 11.8 g
- Carbohydrates 35.6 g
- Sugar 14.4 g
- Protein 5.3 g
- Cholesterol 63 mg

Greek Tomato Basil Bread

Preparation Time: 10 minutes
Cooking Time: 3 hours
Serve: 16

Ingredients:

- 4 cups bread flour
- 2 1/4 tsp active dry yeast
- 2 tbsp parmesan cheese, grated
- 2 cups tomato-basil spaghetti sauce

Directions:

1. Add all ingredients to the bread maker pan.
2. Select the basic bread cycle then select loaf size 2 pound and select crust color medium. Press start.
3. Once done, remove the bread loaf from the bread maker.
4. Let cool bread loaf for 10 minutes.
5. Slice and serve.

Nutritional Value (Amount per Serving):

- Calories 144
- Fat 1.3 g
- Carbohydrates 28.2 g
- Sugar 2.8 g
- Protein 5.1 g
- Cholesterol 3 mg

Flavorful Apricot Bread Loaf

Preparation Time: 10 minutes
Cooking Time: 3 hours
Serve: 16

Ingredients:

- 4 1/4 cups bread flour
- 1/2 cup dried apricots, diced
- 1 3/4 cups orange juice
- 2 tbsp butter, cut into pieces
- 1 tsp ground cinnamon
- 2 tsp active dry yeast
- 1 tbsp sugar
- 2/3 cup rolled oats
- 1 1/2 tsp salt

Directions:

1. Add all ingredients except apricots to the bread maker pan.
2. Select the basic bread cycle then select loaf size 2 pound and select crust color medium. Press start.
3. Add apricots once add ingredient signal beeps.
4. Once done, remove the bread loaf from the bread maker.
5. Let cool bread loaf for 10 minutes.
6. Slice and serve.

Nutritional Value (Amount per Serving):

- Calories 166
- Fat 2.1 g
- Carbohydrates 32 g
- Sugar 3.6 g
- Protein 4.4 g
- Cholesterol 4 mg

Raisin Cinnamon Bread

Preparation Time: 10 minutes
Cooking Time: 2 hours 53 minutes
Serve: 12

Ingredients:

- 3 cups flour
- 3/4 cup raisins
- 2 1/4 tsp instant dry yeast
- 1/3 cup sugar
- 1 tsp ground cinnamon
- 3 tbsp olive oil
- 1 cup of water
- 1 1/2 tsp salt

Directions:

1. Add all ingredients except raisins to the bread maker pan.
2. Select the basic bread cycle then select loaf size 1.5 pound and select crust color medium. Press start.
3. Add raisins once add ingredient signal beeps.
4. Once done, remove the bread loaf from the bread maker.
5. Let cool bread loaf for 10 minutes.
6. Slice and serve.

Nutritional Value (Amount per Serving):

- Calories 192
- Fat 3.9 g
- Carbohydrates 36.7 g
- Sugar 11 g
- Protein 3.5 g
- Cholesterol 0 mg

Blueberry Bread Loaf

Preparation Time: 10 minutes
Cooking Time: 2 hours 53 minutes
Serve: 12

Ingredients:

- 1 egg
- 3 cups bread flour
- 1 tsp active dry yeast
- 1/3 cup dried blueberries
- 1/4 tsp ground nutmeg
- 3 tbsp sugar
- 2 tbsp butter, cut into pieces
- 3 tbsp water
- 3/4 cup milk
- 3/4 tsp salt

Directions:

1. Add all ingredients to the bread maker pan.
2. Select the basic bread cycle then select loaf size 1.5 pound and select crust color medium. Press start.
3. Once done, remove the bread loaf from the bread maker.
4. Let cool bread loaf for 10 minutes.
5. Slice and serve.

Nutritional Value (Amount per Serving):

- Calories 158
- Fat 3 g
- Carbohydrates 28.4 g
- Sugar 4.2 g
- Protein 4.4 g
- Cholesterol 20 mg

Rosemary Olive Bread

Preparation Time: 10 minutes
Cooking Time: 2 hours 53 minutes
Serve: 12

Ingredients:

- 1 cup of water
- 1 cup olives, pitted and quartered
- 1 tbsp sugar
- 2 tbsp olive oil
- 3 1/4 cups bread flour
- 1/4 cup rosemary, chopped
- 1 1/4 tsp instant yeast
- 1 tsp salt

Directions:

1. Add all ingredients except olives to the bread maker pan.
2. Select the basic bread cycle then select loaf size 1.5 pound and select crust color medium. Press start.
3. Add olives once add ingredient signal beeps.
4. Once done, remove the bread loaf from the bread maker.
5. Let cool bread loaf for 10 minutes.
6. Slice and serve.

Nutritional Value (Amount per Serving):

- Calories 165
- Fat 4.1 g
- Carbohydrates 28.5 g
- Sugar 1.1 g
- Protein 3.8 g
- Cholesterol 0 mg

Feta Olives Bread

Preparation Time: 10 minutes
Cooking Time: 3 hours
Serve: 16

Ingredients:

- 3 cups bread flour
- 1/2 cup olives, pitted and chopped
- 1 tbsp sugar
- 2 tsp Active dry yeast
- 3/4 cup feta cheese, crumbled
- 1 cup milk
- 1 tbsp olive oil
- 1 tsp salt

Directions:

1. Add all ingredients to the bread maker pan.
2. Select the basic bread cycle then select loaf size 2 pound and select crust color medium. Press start.
3. Once done, remove the bread loaf from the bread maker.
4. Let cool bread loaf for 10 minutes.
5. Slice and serve.

Nutritional Value (Amount per Serving):

- Calories 128
- Fat 3.4 g
- Carbohydrates 20.1 g
- Sugar 1.8 g
- Protein 4.2 g
- Cholesterol 8 mg

Walnut Blueberry Bread Loaf

Preparation Time: 10 minutes
Cooking Time: 1 hour 40 minutes
Serve: 16

Ingredients:

- 2 eggs
- 2 1/2 cups all-purpose flour
- 1/2 cup walnuts, chopped
- 1 cup frozen blueberries
- 1/2 tsp baking soda
- 2 1/2 tsp baking powder
- 1 cup of sugar
- 1/2 cup milk
- 1/3 cup margarine, softened
- 1 tsp salt

Directions:

1. Add all ingredients except walnuts and blueberries to the bread maker pan.
2. Select the quick bread cycle then select crust color medium. Press start.
3. Add walnuts and blueberries once add ingredient signal beeps.
4. Once done, remove the bread loaf from the bread maker.
5. Let cool bread loaf for 10 minutes.
6. Slice and serve.

Nutritional Value (Amount per Serving):

- Calories 194
- Fat 7 g
- Carbohydrates 29.9 g
- Sugar 13.9 g
- Protein 4 g
- Cholesterol 21 mg

Zucchini Bread

Preparation Time: 10 minutes
Cooking Time: 1 hour 40 minutes
Serve: 12

Ingredients:

- 3 eggs, lightly beaten
- 1 cup zucchini, shredded
- 1/2 tsp allspice
- 1 tsp cinnamon
- 3/4 cup sugar
- 1 tsp baking soda
- 2 tsp baking powder
- 2 cups all-purpose flour
- 1/3 cup olive oil
- 1/2 tsp salt

Directions:

1. Add all ingredients except zucchini to the bread maker pan.
2. Select the quick bread cycle then select crust color medium. Press start.
3. Add zucchini once add ingredient signal beeps.
4. Once done, remove the bread loaf from the bread maker.
5. Let cool bread loaf for 10 minutes.
6. Slice and serve.

Nutritional Value (Amount per Serving):

- Calories 189
- Fat 6.9 g
- Carbohydrates 29.4 g
- Sugar 12.8 g
- Protein 3.7 g
- Cholesterol 41 mg

Pumpkin Walnut Bread

Preparation Time: 10 minutes
Cooking Time: 1 hour 40 minutes
Serve: 16

Ingredients:

- 3 eggs
- 3 cups all-purpose flour
- 1/2 cup walnuts, chopped
- 1/4 tsp ground ginger
- 1/4 tsp ground nutmeg
- 3/4 tsp ground cinnamon
- 1/2 tsp baking soda
- 1 1/2 tsp baking powder
- 1 cup of sugar
- 1 1/2 cups pumpkin puree
- 1/3 cup olive oil
- 1/4 tsp salt

Directions:

1. Add all ingredients except walnuts to the bread maker pan.
2. Select the quick bread cycle then select crust color medium. Press start.
3. Add walnuts once add ingredient signal beeps.
4. Once done, remove the bread loaf from the bread maker.
5. Let cool bread loaf for 10 minutes.
6. Slice and serve.

Nutritional Value (Amount per Serving):

- Calories 213
- Fat 7.6 g
- Carbohydrates 33.1 g
- Sugar 13.4 g
- Protein 4.6 g
- Cholesterol 31 mg

Mushroom Bread

Preparation Time: 10 minutes
Cooking Time: 3 hours
Serve: 16

Ingredients:

- 2 tbsps butter
- 2 cups mushrooms, sliced
- 3/4 cup leek, sliced
- 2 tbsp honey
- 1 1/4 cups Whole wheat flour
- 3 cups bread flour
- 1 tsp yeast
- 1 1/2 tsp dried thyme
- 1 1/3 cups water
- 1 1/2 tsp salt

Directions:

1. Melt butter in a pan over medium-high heat.
2. Add leeks, mushrooms, and thyme and sauté until tender.
3. Transfer mushroom leek mixture into the bread maker pan.
4. Add remaining ingredients into the bread maker pan.
5. Select the basic bread cycle then select loaf size 2 pound and select crust color medium. Press start.
6. Once done, remove the bread loaf from the bread maker.
7. Let cool bread loaf for 10 minutes.
8. Slice and serve.

Nutritional Value (Amount per Serving):

- Calories 147
- Fat 1.8 g
- Carbohydrates 28.6 g
- Sugar 2.6 g
- Protein 3.9 g
- Cholesterol 4 mg

Italian Pesto Bread

Preparation Time: 10 minutes
Cooking Time: 3 hours
Serve: 16

Ingredients:

- 4 cups bread flour
- 1 1/4 tsp bread flour yeast
- 2 tsp garlic, minced
- 1 tbsp sugar
- 1 tbsp dried basil
- 1/2 cup parmesan cheese, shredded
- 1/2 cup parsley, chopped
- 3 tbsp olive oil
- 1 1/4 cups hot water
- 1 1/4 tsp salt

Directions:

1. Add all ingredients to the bread maker pan.
2. Select the basic bread cycle then select loaf size 2 pound and select crust color medium. Press start.
3. Once done, remove the bread loaf from the bread maker.
4. Let cool bread loaf for 10 minutes.
5. Slice and serve.

Nutritional Value (Amount per Serving):

- Calories 151
- Fat 3.6 g
- Carbohydrates 25.3 g
- Sugar 0.9 g
- Protein 4.2 g
- Cholesterol 2 mg

Sweet Potato Bread

Preparation Time: 10 minutes
Cooking Time: 3 hours
Serve: 16

Ingredients:

- 4 cups bread flour
- 1 sweet potato, mashed
- 1/3 cup brown sugar
- 2 tbsp butter, softened
- 1/2 tsp cinnamon
- 1 tsp vanilla
- 1/2 cup warm water
- 2 tbsp milk powder
- 1 1/2 tsp salt

Directions:

1. Add all ingredients into the bread maker pan.
2. Select the basic bread cycle then select loaf size 2 pound and select crust color medium. Press start.
3. Once done, remove the bread loaf from the bread maker.
4. Let cool bread loaf for 10 minutes.
5. Slice and serve.

Nutritional Value (Amount per Serving):

- Calories 149
- Fat 1.8 g
- Carbohydrates 28.9 g
- Sugar 4 g
- Protein 3.8 g
- Cholesterol 4 mg

Banana Walnut Bread

Preparation Time: 10 minutes
Cooking Time: 1 hour 40 minutes
Serve: 12

Ingredients:

- 2 eggs
- 1/2 cup walnuts, chopped
- 1/2 tsp baking soda
- 1 1/4 tsp baking powder
- 2/3 cup sugar
- 1 1/3 cups bread flour
- 2 bananas, mashed
- 1/8 cup milk
- 1/3 cup butter
- 1/2 tsp salt

Directions:

1. Add all ingredients except walnuts to the bread maker pan.
2. Select the quick bread cycle then select crust color medium. Press start.
3. Add walnuts once add ingredient signal beeps.
4. Once done, remove the bread loaf from the bread maker.
5. Let cool bread loaf for 10 minutes.
6. Slice and serve.

Nutritional Value (Amount per Serving):

- Calories 199
- Fat 9.2 g
- Carbohydrates 27.1 g
- Sugar 13.8 g
- Protein 3.9 g
- Cholesterol 41 mg

Chapter 5: Spice & Herb Bread

Delicious Garlic Bread

Preparation Time: 10 minutes
Cooking Time: 1 hour 40 minutes
Serve: 12

Ingredients:

- 2 cups all-purpose flour
- 1 1/2 cups Italian blend cheese, shredded
- 2 tbsp olive oil
- 1 egg, lightly beaten
- 1 cup milk
- 1 tsp dried parsley flakes
- 2 tsp garlic powder
- 1 tbsp sugar
- 4 tsp baking powder
- 1/2 tsp salt

Directions:

1. Add all ingredients to the bread maker pan.
2. Select the quick bread cycle then select crust color medium. Press start.
3. Once done, remove the bread loaf from the bread maker.
4. Let cool bread loaf for 10 minutes.
5. Slice and serve.

Nutritional Value (Amount per Serving):

- Calories 149
- Fat 5.6 g
- Carbohydrates 19.5 g
- Sugar 2.1 g
- Protein 6.1 g
- Cholesterol 21 mg

Caraway Bread

Preparation Time: 10 minutes
Cooking Time: 3 hours
Serve: 12

Ingredients:

- 1 3/4 cups bread flour
- 1 3/4 tsp active dry yeast
- 1 1/2 tbsp caraway seeds
- 3/4 cup rye flour
- 3/4 cup whole wheat flour
- 2 tbsp butter
- 2 tbsp molasses
- 2 tbsp brown sugar
- 2 tsp dry milk powder
- 1 1/4 cups lukewarm water
- 1 tsp salt

Directions:

1. Add all ingredients to the bread maker pan.
2. Select the whole grain bread cycle then select loaf size 2 pound. Press start.
3. Once done, remove the bread loaf from the bread maker.
4. Let cool bread loaf for 10 minutes.
5. Slice and serve.

Nutritional Value (Amount per Serving):

- Calories 159
- Fat 2.6 g
- Carbohydrates 30.2 g
- Sugar 3.7 g
- Protein 4.4 g
- Cholesterol 5 mg

Delicious Herb Bread

Preparation Time: 10 minutes
Cooking Time: 2 hours 53 minutes
Serve: 12

Ingredients:

- 3 cups bread flour
- 1 1/2 tsp yeast
- 1 tsp basil
- 2 tsp thyme
- 2 tsp marjoram
- 2 tsp chives
- 2 tbsp sugar
- 2 tbsp dry milk
- 2 tbsp butter
- 1 1/4 cups water
- 1 1/2 tsp salt

Directions:

1. Add all ingredients to the bread maker pan.
2. Select the sweet bread cycle then select loaf size 1.5 pound and select crust color medium. Press start.
3. Once done, remove the bread loaf from the bread maker.
4. Let cool bread loaf for 10 minutes.
5. Slice and serve.

Nutritional Value (Amount per Serving):

- Calories 142
- Fat 2.3 g
- Carbohydrates 26.3 g
- Sugar 2.2 g
- Protein 3.6 g
- Cholesterol 5 mg

Rosemary Thyme Bread

Preparation Time: 10 minutes
Cooking Time: 2 hours 53 minutes
Serve: 12

Ingredients:

- 3 cups all-purpose flour
- 2 tsp dried rosemary
- 1/2 tsp garlic powder
- 1/2 tsp ground thyme
- 3 tbsp olive oil
- 3 tbsp sugar
- 2 1/2 tsp active dry yeast
- 1 cup of warm water
- 1 1/2 tsp salt

Directions:

1. Add all ingredients to the bread maker pan.
2. Select the basic bread cycle then select loaf size 1.5 pound and select crust color light. Press start.
3. Once done, remove the bread loaf from the bread maker.
4. Let cool bread loaf for 10 minutes.
5. Slice and serve.

Nutritional Value (Amount per Serving):

- Calories 159
- Fat 3.9 g
- Carbohydrates 27.4 g
- Sugar 3.1 g
- Protein 3.6 g
- Cholesterol 0 mg

Rosemary Sun-Dried Tomato Bread

Preparation Time: 10 minutes
Cooking Time: 2 hours 53 minutes
Serve: 12

Ingredients:

- 3 3/4 cups bread flour
- 1 1/4 tsp bread machine yeast
- 1/2 tsp paprika
- 1 tsp dried rosemary
- 2 tbsp sugar
- 2 tbsp olive oil
- 1/3 cup sun-dried tomatoes, chopped
- 1 1/4 cups hot water
- 1 tsp salt

Directions:

1. Add all ingredients to the bread maker pan.
2. Select the sweet bread cycle then select loaf size 1.5 pound and select crust color medium. Press start.
3. Once done, remove the bread loaf from the bread maker.
4. Let cool bread loaf for 10 minutes.
5. Slice and serve.

Nutritional Value (Amount per Serving):

- Calories 172
- Fat 2.8 g
- Carbohydrates 32.3 g
- Sugar 2.3 g
- Protein 4.2 g
- Cholesterol 0 mg

Rosemary Thyme Orange Bread

Preparation Time: 10 minutes
Cooking Time: 2 hours 53 minutes
Serve: 12

Ingredients:

- 2 eggs
- 3 drops orange essential oil
- 2 1/4 tsp yeast
- 1/2 tsp parsley, chopped
- 1 tsp thyme, chopped
- 1 tsp rosemary, chopped
- 2/3 cup milk
- 1 1/2 tbsp olive oil
- 2 1/2 tbsp sugar
- 3 cups flour
- 1 1/2 tsp salt

Directions:

1. Add all ingredients to the bread maker pan.
2. Select the sweet bread cycle then select loaf size 1.5 pound and select crust color medium. Press start.
3. Once done, remove the bread loaf from the bread maker.
4. Let cool bread loaf for 10 minutes.
5. Slice and serve.

Nutritional Value (Amount per Serving):

- Calories 158
- Fat 3.1 g
- Carbohydrates 27.5 g
- Sugar 3.3 g
- Protein 4.9 g
- Cholesterol 28 mg

Cinnamon Bread

Preparation Time: 10 minutes
Cooking Time: 2 hours 53 minutes
Serve: 12

Ingredients:

- 3 1/2 cups bread flour
- 2 tsp bread machine yeast
- 1 1/2 tsp cinnamon
- 2 tbsp olive oil
- 2 tbsp dry milk
- 1/4 cup sugar
- 1 cup of water
- 1 1/2 tsp salt

Directions:

1. Add all ingredients to the bread maker pan.
2. Select the basic bread cycle then select loaf size 1.5 pound and select crust color light. Press start.
3. Once done, remove the bread loaf from the bread maker.
4. Let cool bread loaf for 10 minutes.
5. Slice and serve.

Nutritional Value (Amount per Serving):

- Calories 172
- Fat 2.8 g
- Carbohydrates 32.6 g
- Sugar 4.4 g
- Protein 4.1 g
- Cholesterol 0 mg

Herb French Bread

Preparation Time: 10 minutes
Cooking Time: 3 hours 40 minutes
Serve: 12

Ingredients:

- 3 cups all-purpose flour
- 2 1/2 tsp instant dry yeast
- 3 tbsp sugar
- 1/2 tsp garlic powder
- 1 cup of warm water
- 1/2 tsp dried oregano
- 1/2 tsp dried basil
- 1/8 tsp dried thyme
- 1 tsp dried rosemary
- 3 tbsp olive oil
- 1 1/2 tsp sea salt

Directions:

1. Add all ingredients to the bread maker pan.
2. Select the French bread cycle then select loaf size 1.5 pound and select crust color medium. Press start.
3. Once done, remove the bread loaf from the bread maker.
4. Let cool bread loaf for 10 minutes.
5. Slice and serve.

Nutritional Value (Amount per Serving):

- Calories 156
- Fat 3.8 g
- Carbohydrates 27.1 g
- Sugar 3.1 g
- Protein 3.3 g
- Cholesterol 0 mg

Flavors Herb Bread

Preparation Time: 10 minutes
Cooking Time: 2 hours 53 minutes
Serve: 12

Ingredients:

- 3 1/2 cups bread flour
- 2 tsp active dry yeast
- 1 tsp dried oregano
- 2 tbsp dried parsley flakes
- 2 tbsp sugar
- 1/4 cup dried onion, minced
- 2 tbsp butter, softened
- 1 egg, lightly beaten
- 1 cup warm milk
- 1 1/2 tsp salt

Directions:

1. Add all ingredients to the bread maker pan.
2. Select the basic bread cycle then select loaf size 1.5 pound and select crust color light. Press start.
3. Once done, remove the bread loaf from the bread maker.
4. Let cool bread loaf for 10 minutes.
5. Slice and serve.

Nutritional Value (Amount per Serving):

- Calories 176
- Fat 3.1 g
- Carbohydrates 31.5 g
- Sugar 3.2 g
- Protein 5.2 g
- Cholesterol 20 mg

Tomato Rosemary Bread

Preparation Time: 10 minutes
Cooking Time: 2 hours 53 minutes
Serve: 12

Ingredients:

- 2 cups bread flour
- 1/4 cup sun-dried tomato, chopped
- 2 tsp yeast
- 1/3 cup parmesan cheese, grated
- 1 tbsp fresh rosemary, chopped
- 1 tsp sugar
- 2 tbsp olive oil
- 1/4 cup milk
- 1/2 cup water
- 1 tsp salt

Directions:

1. Add all ingredients except tomato to the bread maker pan.
2. Select the sweet bread cycle then select loaf size 1.5 pound and select crust color medium. Press start.
3. Add tomato once add ingredient signal beeps.
4. Once done, remove the bread loaf from the bread maker.
5. Let cool bread loaf for 10 minutes.
6. Slice and serve.

Nutritional Value (Amount per Serving):

- Calories 115
- Fat 3.6 g
- Carbohydrates 17.5 g
- Sugar 0.6 g
- Protein 3.5 g
- Cholesterol 2 mg

Herb Zucchini Bread

Preparation Time: 10 minutes
Cooking Time: 2 hours 53 minutes
Serve: 12

Ingredients:

- 2 cups bread flour
- 1 1/2 tsp active dry yeast
- 2 tsp sesame seeds
- 1 tbsp fresh basil, chopped
- 3/4 cup whole wheat flour
- 3/4 cup zucchini, grated
- 1 tbsp olive oil
- 2 tsp honey
- 1/2 cup water
- 1 tsp salt

Directions:

1. Add all ingredients to the bread maker pan.
2. Select the sweet bread cycle then select loaf size 1.5 pound and select crust color medium. Press start.
3. Once done, remove the bread loaf from the bread maker.
4. Let cool bread loaf for 10 minutes.
5. Slice and serve.

Nutritional Value (Amount per Serving):

- Calories 123
- Fat 1.7 g
- Carbohydrates 23.4 g
- Sugar 1.2 g
- Protein 3.3 g
- Cholesterol 0 mg

Greek Herb Bread

Preparation Time: 10 minutes
Cooking Time: 3 hours
Serve: 16

Ingredients:

- 4 cups all-purpose flour
- 1 packet active dry yeast
- 4 tsp dried Italian seasoning
- 3 tbsp sugar
- 1/3 cup olive oil
- 1 1/3 cup water
- 2 tsp salt

Directions:

1. Add all ingredients to the bread maker pan.
2. Select the basic bread cycle then select loaf size 2 pound and select crust color medium. Press start.
3. Once done, remove the bread loaf from the bread maker.
4. Let cool bread loaf for 10 minutes.
5. Slice and serve.

Nutritional Value (Amount per Serving):

- Calories 163
- Fat 4.9 g
- Carbohydrates 26.4 g
- Sugar 2.4 g
- Protein 3.4 g
- Cholesterol 1 mg

Dill Pepper Bread

Preparation Time: 10 minutes
Cooking Time: 58 minutes
Serve: 12

Ingredients:

- 3 cups bread flour
- 3 tsp instant yeast
- 2 tbsp dry milk
- 2 tbsp olive oil
- 3 tbsp sugar
- 1/2 tsp dried dill weed
- 1/2 tsp pepper
- 1 cup of warm water
- 1 tsp salt

Directions:

1. Add all ingredients to the bread maker pan.
2. Select the express bread cycle then select loaf size 1.5 pound and select crust color dark. Press start.
3. Once done, remove the bread loaf from the bread maker.
4. Let cool bread loaf for 10 minutes.
5. Slice and serve.

Nutritional Value (Amount per Serving):

- Calories 150
- Fat 2.7 g
- Carbohydrates 27.4 g
- Sugar 3.2 g
- Protein 3.7 g
- Cholesterol 0 mg

Jalapeno Bread

Preparation Time: 10 minutes
Cooking Time: 2 hours 53 minutes
Serve: 12

Ingredients:

- 2 cups bread flour
- 8 tbsp jalapeno pepper, chopped
- 1/3 cup Monterey jack cheese, shredded
- 1 1/2 tbsp sugar
- 3/4 cup warm water
- 1 1/4 tsp active dry yeast
- 3/4 tsp salt

Directions:

1. Add all ingredients to the bread maker pan.
2. Select the sweet bread cycle then select loaf size 1.5 pound and select crust color medium. Press start.
3. Once done, remove the bread loaf from the bread maker.
4. Let cool bread loaf for 10 minutes.
5. Slice and serve.

Nutritional Value (Amount per Serving):

- Calories 96
- Fat 1.2 g
- Carbohydrates 17.8 g
- Sugar 1.7 g
- Protein 3.1 g
- Cholesterol 3 mg

Cajun Bread

Preparation Time: 10 minutes
Cooking Time: 2 hours 53 minutes
Serve: 12

Ingredients:

- 2 cups bread flour
- 1 tsp active dry yeast
- 1 tsp Cajun seasoning
- 1 tbsp sugar
- 2 tsp butter, softened
- 2 tsp garlic, chopped
- 1/4 cup green bell pepper, chopped
- 1/4 cup onion, chopped
- 1/2 cup water
- 1/2 tsp salt

Directions:

1. Add all ingredients to the bread maker pan.
2. Select the sweet bread cycle then select loaf size 1.5 pound and select crust color dark. Press start.
3. Once done, remove the bread loaf from the bread maker.
4. Let cool bread loaf for 10 minutes.
5. Slice and serve.

Nutritional Value (Amount per Serving):

- Calories 89
- Fat 0.9 g
- Carbohydrates 17.6 g
- Sugar 1.3 g
- Protein 2.4 g
- Cholesterol 2 mg

Tasty Dill Pickle Bread

Preparation Time: 10 minutes
Cooking Time: 2 hours 53 minutes
Serve: 12

Ingredients:

- 3 1/8 cups bread flour
- 2 tsp active dry yeast
- 1/2 tsp dried dill weed
- 1 tsp dried parsley
- 1 tbsp dried onion, minced
- 1 tbsp butter, softened
- 1 dill pickle, chopped
- 1 cup of warm water
- 1/4 tsp salt

Directions:

1. Add all ingredients to the bread maker pan.
2. Select the sweet bread cycle then select loaf size 1.5 pound and select crust color medium. Press start.
3. Once done, remove the bread loaf from the bread maker.
4. Let cool bread loaf for 10 minutes.
5. Slice and serve.

Nutritional Value (Amount per Serving):

- Calories 130
- Fat 1.3 g
- Carbohydrates 25.3 g
- Sugar 0.2 g
- Protein 3.7 g
- Cholesterol 3 mg

Chapter 6: Cheese Bread

Pepperoni Cheese Bread

Preparation Time: 10 minutes
Cooking Time: 2 hours 53 minutes
Serve: 12

Ingredients:

- 2/3 cup pepperoni, diced
- 1 1/2 tsp active dry yeast
- 3 1/4 cups bread flour
- 1 1/2 tsp dried oregano
- 2 tbsp sugar
- 1/3 cup mozzarella cheese, shredded
- 1 cup+2 tbsp warm water
- 1 1/2 tsp garlic salt

Directions:

1. Add all ingredients except pepperoni to the bread maker pan.
2. Select the sweet bread cycle then select loaf size 1.5 pound and select crust color medium. Press start.
3. Add pepperoni once add ingredient signal beeps.
4. Once done, remove the bread loaf from the bread maker.
5. Let cool bread loaf for 10 minutes.
6. Slice and serve.

Nutritional Value (Amount per Serving):

- Calories 164
- Fat 3 g
- Carbohydrates 28.4 g
- Sugar 2.2 g
- Protein 5.3 g
- Cholesterol 28.4 mg

Basil Garlic Parmesan Bread

Preparation Time: 10 minutes
Cooking Time: 2 hours 53 minutes
Serve: 12

Ingredients:

- 3 1/2 cups all-purpose flour
- 1 tbsp garlic, minced
- 1/4 oz active dry yeast
- 3 tbsp sugar
- 2 tsp kosher salt
- 1 tsp dried oregano
- 1 tsp dried basil
- 1/2 tsp garlic powder
- 1/2 cup parmesan cheese, grated
- 1/4 cup butter, melted
- 1/3 cup olive oil
- 1 1/3 cups water

Directions:

1. Add all ingredients to the bread maker pan.
2. Select the basic bread cycle then select loaf size 1.5 pound and select crust color medium. Press start.
3. Once done, remove the bread loaf from the bread maker.
4. Let cool bread loaf for 10 minutes.
5. Slice and serve.

Nutritional Value (Amount per Serving):

- Calories 242
- Fat 10.6 g
- Carbohydrates 31.6 g
- Sugar 3.2 g
- Protein 5.3 g
- Cholesterol 13 mg

Easy Cheese Jalapeno Bread

Preparation Time: 10 minutes
Cooking Time: 2 hours 53 minutes
Serve: 12

Ingredients:

- 1/4 cup Monterey jack cheese, shredded
- 2 tsp active dry yeast
- 1 1/2 tbsp butter
- 1 1/2 tbsp sugar
- 3 tbsp milk
- 3 cups flour
- 1 cup of water
- 1 jalapeno pepper, minced
- 1 1/2 tsp salt

Directions:

1. Add all ingredients to the bread maker pan.
2. Select the basic bread cycle then select loaf size 1.5 pound and select crust color medium. Press start.
3. Once done, remove the bread loaf from the bread maker.
4. Let cool bread loaf for 10 minutes.
5. Slice and serve.

Nutritional Value (Amount per Serving):

- Calories 145
- Fat 2.6 g
- Carbohydrates 25.9 g
- Sugar 1.8 g
- Protein 4.2 g
- Cholesterol 6 mg

Pepper Jack Cheese Bread

Preparation Time: 10 minutes
Cooking Time: 2 hours 53 minutes
Serve: 12

Ingredients:

- 3 cups bread flour
- 2 tsp active dry yeast
- 2 tbsp brown sugar
- 2 tbsp parmesan cheese, grated
- 1 tsp pepper
- 2 tsp Italian seasoning
- 1/2 cup pepper jack cheese, shredded
- 1 1/4 cups warm water
- 1 1/2 tsp salt

Directions:

1. Add all ingredients to the bread maker pan.
2. Select the basic bread cycle then select loaf size 1.5 pound and select crust color medium. Press start.
3. Once done, remove the bread loaf from the bread maker.
4. Let cool bread loaf for 10 minutes.
5. Slice and serve.

Nutritional Value (Amount per Serving):

- Calories 145
- Fat 2.2 g
- Carbohydrates 25.9 g
- Sugar 1.6 g
- Protein 5.1 g
- Cholesterol 6 mg

Healthy Cheese Bread

Preparation Time: 10 minutes
Cooking Time: 2 hours 53 minutes
Serve: 12

Ingredients:

- 3 eggs
- 2 cups white rice flour
- 1 cup brown rice flour
- 1/4 cup milk powder
- 2 tbsp sugar
- 1 tbsp poppy seeds
- 2 tbsp olive oil
- 1 1/2 cups water
- 2 1/4 tsp active dry yeast
- 3 1/2 tsp Xanthan gum
- 1 1/2 cups cheddar cheese, shredded
- 1 tsp salt

Directions:

1. Add all ingredients to the bread maker pan.
2. Select the basic bread cycle then select loaf size 1.5 pound and select crust color medium. Press start.
3. Once done, remove the bread loaf from the bread maker.
4. Let cool bread loaf for 10 minutes.
5. Slice and serve.

Nutritional Value (Amount per Serving):

- Calories 261
- Fat 9.2 g
- Carbohydrates 36.7 g
- Sugar 3.7 g
- Protein 9 g
- Cholesterol 56 mg

Buttermilk Cheese Bread

Preparation Time: 10 minutes
Cooking Time: 2 hours 53 minutes
Serve: 12

Ingredients:

- 3 cups bread flour
- 1 1/8 cups buttermilk
- 1 1/2 tsp active dry yeast
- 3/4 cup cheddar cheese, shredded
- 1 1/2 tsp sugar
- 1 1/8 cups buttermilk
- 1 1/2 tsp salt

Directions:

1. Add all ingredients to the bread maker pan.
2. Select the basic bread cycle then select loaf size 1.5 pound and select crust color medium. Press start.
3. Once done, remove the bread loaf from the bread maker.
4. Let cool bread loaf for 10 minutes.
5. Slice and serve.

Nutritional Value (Amount per Serving):

- Calories 164
- Fat 3.1 g
- Carbohydrates 26.8 g
- Sugar 2.8 g
- Protein 6.7 g
- Cholesterol 9 mg

Italian Cheddar Cheese Bread

Preparation Time: 10 minutes
Cooking Time: 2 hours 53 minutes
Serve: 12

Ingredients:

- 3 cups bread flour
- 4 tbsp butter
- 1 1/2 tsp yeast
- 1 tbsp Italian herb seasoning
- 2 tbsp brown sugar
- 1 cup cheddar cheese, shredded
- 1 1/4 cups warm milk
- 2 tsp salt

Directions:

1. Add all ingredients to the bread maker pan.
2. Select the basic bread cycle then select loaf size 1.5 pound and select crust color medium. Press start.
3. Once done, remove the bread loaf from the bread maker.
4. Let cool bread loaf for 10 minutes.
5. Slice and serve.

Nutritional Value (Amount per Serving):

- Calories 206
- Fat 7.8 g
- Carbohydrates 26.9 g
- Sugar 2.7 g
- Protein 6.6 g
- Cholesterol 22 mg

Cheddar Cheese Bread

Preparation Time: 10 minutes
Cooking Time: 2 hours 53 minutes
Serve: 12

Ingredients:

- 1 cup milk
- 1/2 cup butter, melted
- 3 cups all-purpose flour
- 1 tbsp sugar
- 1 1/4 oz active dry yeast
- 2 cups cheddar cheese, shredded
- 1/2 tsp garlic powder
- 2 tsp kosher salt

Directions:

1. Add all ingredients to the bread maker pan.
2. Select the basic bread cycle then select loaf size 1.5 pound and select crust color medium. Press start.
3. Once done, remove the bread loaf from the bread maker.
4. Let cool bread loaf for 10 minutes.
5. Slice and serve.

Nutritional Value (Amount per Serving):

- Calories 280
- Fat 14.8 g
- Carbohydrates 27.3 g
- Sugar 2.1 g
- Protein 9.8 g
- Cholesterol 42 mg

Basil Oregano Thyme Cheese Bread

Preparation Time: 10 minutes
Cooking Time: 2 hours 53 minutes
Serve: 12

Ingredients:

- 3 cups bread flour
- 1 tbsp active dry yeast
- 1 tsp dried oregano
- 1 tsp dried basil
- 1 1/2 tsp dried thyme
- 1 1/2 tsp dried marjoram
- 3 tbsp parmesan cheese, grated
- 2 tbsp butter, softened
- 2 tbsp sugar
- 2 tbsp milk powder
- 1 1/4 cups warm water
- 1 1/2 tsp salt

Directions:

1. Add all ingredients to the bread maker pan.
2. Select the basic bread cycle then select loaf size 1.5 pound and select crust color medium. Press start.
3. Once done, remove the bread loaf from the bread maker.
4. Let cool bread loaf for 10 minutes.
5. Slice and serve.

Nutritional Value (Amount per Serving):

- Calories 154
- Fat 2.7 g
- Carbohydrates 27.2 g
- Sugar 2.8 g
- Protein 4.8 g
- Cholesterol 7 mg

Easy Cheesy Bread Loaf

Preparation Time: 10 minutes
Cooking Time: 2 hours 53 minutes
Serve: 12

Ingredients:

- 1 egg
- 1 tsp bread machine yeast
- 2 tbsp sugar
- 2 tbsp dry milk
- 1 cup sharp cheddar cheese, shredded
- 3 cups bread flour
- 3/4 cup water
- 1 tsp salt

Directions:

1. Add all ingredients to the bread maker pan.
2. Select the basic bread cycle then select loaf size 1.5 pound and select crust color medium. Press start.
3. Once done, remove the bread loaf from the bread maker.
4. Let cool bread loaf for 10 minutes.
5. Slice and serve.

Nutritional Value (Amount per Serving):

- Calories 167
- Fat 3.9 g
- Carbohydrates 26.3 g
- Sugar 2.3 g
- Protein 6.3 g
- Cholesterol 24 mg

Cranberry Cream Cheese Bread

Preparation Time: 10 minutes
Cooking Time: 2 hours 53 minutes
Serve: 12

Ingredients:

- 4 eggs
- 2 cups cranberries
- 1 1/2 tsp baking powder
- 2 cups all-purpose flour
- 1 1/2 tsp vanilla
- 1 1/2 cups sugar
- 8 oz cream cheese, softened
- 1 cup butter, softened
- 1/2 tsp salt

Directions:

1. Add all ingredients to the bread maker pan.
2. Select the basic bread cycle then select loaf size 1.5 pound and select crust color medium. Press start.
3. Once done, remove the bread loaf from the bread maker.
4. Let cool bread loaf for 10 minutes.
5. Slice and serve.

Nutritional Value (Amount per Serving):

- Calories 404
- Fat 23.6 g
- Carbohydrates 43.6 g
- Sugar 26 g
- Protein 5.6 g
- Cholesterol 116 mg

Cream Cheese Bread

Preparation Time: 10 minutes
Cooking Time: 2 hours 53 minutes
Serve: 12

Ingredients:

- 1 egg
- 2 1/2 tsp active dry yeast
- 3 cups bread flour
- 3 tbsp sugar
- 1/4 cup margarine
- 1 cup cream cheese, diced
- 1/3 cup milk
- 1 tsp salt

Directions:

1. Add all ingredients to the bread maker pan.
2. Select the basic bread cycle then select loaf size 1.5 pound and select crust color light. Press start.
3. Once done, remove the bread loaf from the bread maker.
4. Let cool bread loaf for 10 minutes.
5. Slice and serve.

Nutritional Value (Amount per Serving):

- Calories 237
- Fat 11.4 g
- Carbohydrates 28.1 g
- Sugar 3.5 g
- Protein 5.7 g
- Cholesterol 35 mg

Cheese Beer Bread

Preparation Time: 10 minutes
Cooking Time: 2 hours 53 minutes
Serve: 12

Ingredients:

- 3 cups bread flour
- 1 packet active dry yeast
- 4 oz American cheese, shredded
- 10 oz beer
- 1 tbsp butter
- 4 oz Monterey Jack cheese, shredded
- 1 tbsp sugar
- 1 1/2 tsp salt

Directions:

1. Add all ingredients to the bread maker pan.
2. Select the basic bread cycle then select loaf size 1.5 pound and select crust color light. Press start.
3. Once done, remove the bread loaf from the bread maker.
4. Let cool bread loaf for 10 minutes.
5. Slice and serve.

Nutritional Value (Amount per Serving):

- Calories 204
- Fat 6.5 g
- Carbohydrates 26.7 g
- Sugar 1.8 g
- Protein 7.6 g
- Cholesterol 19 mg

Asiago Cheese Bread

Preparation Time: 10 minutes
Cooking Time: 2 hours 53 minutes
Serve: 12

Ingredients:

- 1 1/3 cups Asiago cheese, shredded
- 2 tbsp butter
- 1 1/4 cups milk
- 1/4 tsp pepper
- 1 tsp sugar
- 2 1/4 tsp yeast
- 3 1/4 cups all-purpose flour
- 1 1/2 tsp salt

Directions:

1. Add all ingredients to the bread maker pan.
2. Select the basic bread cycle then select loaf size 1.5 pound and select crust color light. Press start.
3. Once done, remove the bread loaf from the bread maker.
4. Let cool bread loaf for 10 minutes.
5. Slice and serve.

Nutritional Value (Amount per Serving):

- Calories 194
- Fat 5.8 g
- Carbohydrates 27.7 g
- Sugar 1.6 g
- Protein 7.3 g
- Cholesterol 16 mg

Parmesan Herb Bread

Preparation Time: 10 minutes
Cooking Time: 2 hours 53 minutes
Serve: 12

Ingredients:

- 3 1/2 cups bread flour
- 1 1/2 tsp bread machine yeast
- 3 tbsp parmesan cheese, grated
- 1 tsp dried oregano, crushed
- 1 tsp dried basil
- 3 tbsp olive oil
- 1 tbsp sugar
- 1 cup of water
- 1 1/8 tsp salt

Directions:

1. Add all ingredients to the bread maker pan.
2. Select the basic bread cycle then select loaf size 1.5 pound and select crust color medium. Press start.
3. Once done, remove the bread loaf from the bread maker.
4. Let cool bread loaf for 10 minutes.
5. Slice and serve.

Nutritional Value (Amount per Serving):

- Calories 175
- Fat 4.3 g
- Carbohydrates 29.2 g
- Sugar 1.1 g
- Protein 4.6 g
- Cholesterol 1 mg

Easy Cheddar Bread

Preparation Time: 10 minutes
Cooking Time: 2 hours 53 minutes
Serve: 12

Ingredients:

- 3 1/4 cup bread flour
- 3 tsp bread machine yeast
- 1/3 cup cheddar cheese, grated
- 2 tbsp dry milk
- 2 tbsp olive oil
- 3 tbsp sugar
- 1 cup of warm water
- 1 tsp salt

Directions:

1. Add all ingredients to the bread maker pan.
2. Select the basic bread cycle then select loaf size 1.5 pound and select crust color medium. Press start.
3. Once done, remove the bread loaf from the bread maker.
4. Let cool bread loaf for 10 minutes.
5. Slice and serve.

Nutritional Value (Amount per Serving):

- Calories 171
- Fat 3.8 g
- Carbohydrates 29.4 g
- Sugar 3.2 g
- Protein 4.7 g
- Cholesterol 4 mg

Chapter 7: Sweet Bread

Portuguese Bread

Preparation Time: 10 minutes
Cooking Time: 2 hours 55 minutes
Serve: 16

Ingredients:

- 2 eggs
- 2 tsp vanilla
- 1 egg yolk
- 1 lemon zest
- 1 tbsp instant yeast
- 3 1/4 cups all-purpose flour
- 1/3 cup sugar
- 4 tbsp butter, cut into pieces
- 1/2 cup milk
- 1 1/4 tsp salt

Directions:

1. Add all ingredients to the bread maker pan.
2. Select the sweet bread cycle then select loaf size 2 pound and select crust color medium. Press start.
3. Once done, remove the bread loaf from the bread maker.
4. Let cool bread loaf for 10 minutes.
5. Slice and serve.

Nutritional Value (Amount per Serving):

- Calories 152
- Fat 4.2 g
- Carbohydrates 24.7 g
- Sugar 4.8 g
- Protein 4.1 g
- Cholesterol 42 mg

Nut Banana Bread Loaf

Preparation Time: 10 minutes
Cooking Time: 1 hour 40 minutes
Serve: 12

Ingredients:

- 14 oz banana quick bread mix
- 1/4 cup walnuts, chopped
- 1/4 cup mixed nuts, chopped
- 2 eggs, lightly beaten
- 1/4 cup olive oil
- 1 cup of water

Directions:

1. Add all ingredients except mixed nuts and walnuts to the bread maker pan.
2. Select the quick bread cycle then select crust color light. Press start.
3. Add mixed nuts and walnuts once add ingredient signal beeps.
4. Once done, remove the bread loaf from the bread maker.
5. Let cool bread loaf for 10 minutes.
6. Slice and serve.

Nutritional Value (Amount per Serving):

- Calories 221
- Fat 10.9 g
- Carbohydrates 27.5 g
- Sugar 14.2 g
- Protein 3.6 g
- Cholesterol 27 mg

Cinnamon Apple Bread

Preparation Time: 10 minutes
Cooking Time: 2 hours 50 minutes
Serve: 12

Ingredients:

- 3 cups flour
- 2 1/2 tsp bread machine yeast
- 1/2 tsp cinnamon
- 3 tbsp sugar
- 2 apples, peel & dice
- 2 tbsp butter, melted
- 1 cup warm milk
- 1 1/2 tsp salt

Directions:

1. Add apple and 1 tbsp sugar to the mixing bowl and set aside for 30 minutes.
2. Add all ingredients to the bread maker pan.
3. Select the sweet bread cycle then select loaf size 1.5 pound and select crust color medium. Press start.
4. Once done, remove the bread loaf from the bread maker.
5. Let cool bread loaf for 10 minutes.
6. Slice and serve.

Nutritional Value (Amount per Serving):

- Calories 174
- Fat 2.8 g
- Carbohydrates 33.4 g
- Sugar 7.9 g
- Protein 4.3 g
- Cholesterol 7 mg

Cranberry Cinnamon Bread

Preparation Time: 10 minutes
Cooking Time: 2 hours 50 minutes
Serve: 12

Ingredients:

- 3 1/2 cups bread flour
- 2 1/4 tsp dry yeast
- 1 cup dried cranberries
- 1 1/2 tsp cinnamon
- 1 1/4 cups water
- 2 tbsp butter
- 2 1/2 tbsp sugar
- 1 tsp salt

Directions:

1. Add all ingredients except cranberries and cinnamon to the bread maker pan in the listed order.
2. Select the sweet bread cycle then select loaf size 1.5 pound and select crust color light. Press start.
3. Add cinnamon and cranberries once add ingredient signal beeps.
4. Once done, remove the bread loaf from the bread maker.
5. Let cool bread loaf for 10 minutes.
6. Slice and serve.

Nutritional Value (Amount per Serving):

- Calories 167
- Fat 2.3 g
- Carbohydrates 31.7 g
- Sugar 2.9 g
- Protein 4.1 g
- Cholesterol 5 mg

Sweet Honey Whole Wheat Bread

Preparation Time: 10 minutes
Cooking Time: 3 hours
Serve: 16

Ingredients:

- 1 cup whole wheat flour
- 2 tsp bread machine yeast
- 1 cup granola
- 2 1/2 cups bread flour
- 2 tbsp olive oil
- 1/4 cup honey
- 1 1/2 cups water
- 1 1/2 tsp salt

Directions:

1. Add all ingredients to the bread maker pan.
2. Select the basic bread cycle then select loaf size 2 pound and select crust color medium. Press start.
3. Once done, remove the bread loaf from the bread maker.
4. Let cool bread loaf for 10 minutes.
5. Slice and serve.

Nutritional Value (Amount per Serving):

- Calories 199
- Fat 7.6 g
- Carbohydrates 44.7 g
- Sugar 10 g
- Protein 7.1 g
- Cholesterol 0 mg

Buttermilk Apple Bread

Preparation Time: 10 minutes
Cooking Time: 2 hours 50 minutes
Serve: 12

Ingredients:

- 3 1/2 cups bread flour
- 4 tsp vital wheat gluten
- 1 cup buttermilk
- 3 tbsp brown sugar
- 1 1/2 tsp ground cinnamon
- 1 cup apple, peeled and chopped
- 1/4 cup apple juice concentrate
- 1 1/2 tbsp butter
- 2 tsp yeast
- 1 tsp salt

Directions:

1. Add all ingredients to the bread maker pan.
2. Select the sweet bread cycle then select loaf size 1.5 pound and select crust color light. Press start.
3. Once done, remove the bread loaf from the bread maker.
4. Let cool bread loaf for 10 minutes.
5. Slice and serve.

Nutritional Value (Amount per Serving):

- Calories 190
- Fat 2.1 g
- Carbohydrates 36.3 g
- Sugar 6.9 g
- Protein 6.4 g
- Cholesterol 5 mg

Delicious Pumpkin Bread

Preparation Time: 10 minutes
Cooking Time: 1 hour 40 minutes
Serve: 12

Ingredients:

- 3 eggs
- 3 cups all-purpose flour
- 1/4 tsp ground ginger
- 1/4 tsp ground nutmeg
- 3/4 tsp ground cinnamon
- 1/2 tsp baking soda
- 1 1/2 tsp baking powder
- 1 cup of sugar
- 1 1/2 cups pumpkin puree
- 1/3 cup olive oil
- 1/4 tsp salt

Directions:

1. Add all ingredients to the bread maker pan.
2. Select the quick bread cycle then select crust color medium. Press start.
3. Once done, remove the bread loaf from the bread maker.
4. Let cool bread loaf for 10 minutes.
5. Slice and serve.

Nutritional Value (Amount per Serving):

- Calories 252
- Fat 7.1 g
- Carbohydrates 43.5 g
- Sugar 17.9 g
- Protein 5 g
- Cholesterol 41 mg

Cranberry Bread

Preparation Time: 10 minutes
Cooking Time: 2 hours 50 minutes
Serve: 12

Ingredients:

- 3 1/2 cups bread flour
- 1/3 cup pecans, chopped
- 2 tsp bread machine yeast
- 1 1/2 tsp vanilla
- 2 tbsp butter, cut into pieces
- 2 tbsp dry milk
- 1/4 cup sugar
- 1/3 cup dried cranberries
- 1/4 cup orange juice
- 3/4 cup water
- 1 1/2 tsp salt

Directions:

1. Add all ingredients except pecans and cranberries to the bread maker pan.
2. Select the sweet bread cycle then select loaf size 1.5 pound and select crust color light. Press start.
3. Add pecans and cranberries once add ingredient signal beeps.
4. Once done, remove the bread loaf from the bread maker.
5. Let cool bread loaf for 10 minutes.
6. Slice and serve.

Nutritional Value (Amount per Serving):

- Calories 192
- Fat 4.2 g
- Carbohydrates 33.6 g
- Sugar 5.1 g
- Protein 4.4 g
- Cholesterol 5 mg

Chocolate Chip Bread

Preparation Time: 10 minutes
Cooking Time: 2 hours 50 minutes
Serve: 12

Ingredients:

- 1 egg, lightly beaten
- 1 cup warm milk
- 1/4 cup water
- 1 1/2 tsp yeast
- 3 cups bread flour
- 2 tbsp brown sugar
- 2 tbsp sugar
- 1 tsp salt
- 1 tsp cinnamon
- 4 tbsp butter, softened
- 1 cup of chocolate chips

Directions:

1. Add all ingredients except chocolate chips to the bread maker pan.
2. Select the sweet bread cycle then select loaf size 1.5 pound and select crust color light. Press start.
3. Add chocolate chips once add ingredient signal beeps.
4. Once done, remove the bread loaf from the bread maker.
5. Let cool bread loaf for 10 minutes.
6. Slice and serve.

Nutritional Value (Amount per Serving):

- Calories 253
- Fat 9.1 g
- Carbohydrates 37 g
- Sugar 11.7 g
- Protein 5.7 g
- Cholesterol 29 mg

Choco Chip Pumpkin Bread

Preparation Time: 10 minutes
Cooking Time: 2 hours 50 minutes
Serve: 12

Ingredients:

- 2 eggs
- 1/3 cup chocolate chips
- 1 1/2 cups brown sugar
- 1/2 cup olive oil
- 15 oz can pumpkin puree
- 1/2 tsp baking powder
- 1 tsp baking soda
- 1 tsp cinnamon
- 2 tsp pumpkin pie spice
- 2 cups all-purpose flour
- 1/2 tsp salt

Directions:

1. Add all ingredients except chocolate chips to the bread maker pan.
2. Select the sweet bread cycle then select loaf size 1.5 pound and select crust color medium. Press start.
3. Add chocolate chips once add ingredient signal beeps.
4. Once done, remove the bread loaf from the bread maker.
5. Let cool bread loaf for 10 minutes.
6. Slice and serve.

Nutritional Value (Amount per Serving):

- Calories 306
- Fat 10.8 g
- Carbohydrates 49.5 g
- Sugar 25.1 g
- Protein 4.7 g
- Cholesterol 28 mg

Chocolate Bread

Preparation Time: 10 minutes
Cooking Time: 2 hours 50 minutes
Serve: 12

Ingredients:

- 1 egg
- 1 egg yolk
- 3 tbsp olive oil
- 1 tsp vanilla extract
- 1 cup milk
- 3 cups bread flour
- 1/2 cup brown sugar
- 1/3 cup cocoa powder
- 1 tbsp vital wheat gluten
- 2 1/2 tsp yeast
- 1 tsp salt

Directions:

1. Add all ingredients to the bread maker pan.
2. Select the sweet bread cycle then select loaf size 1.5 pound and select crust color light. Press start.
3. Once done, remove the bread loaf from the bread maker.
4. Let cool bread loaf for 10 minutes.
5. Slice and serve.

Nutritional Value (Amount per Serving):

- Calories 201
- Fat 5.4 g
- Carbohydrates 32.8 g
- Sugar 7 g
- Protein 6.5 g
- Cholesterol 33 mg

Coffee Bread

Preparation Time: 10 minutes
Cooking Time: 2 hours 50 minutes
Serve: 12

Ingredients:

- 3 cups bread flour
- 2 1/2 tsp active dry yeast
- 1/4 tsp ground cloves
- 1/4 tsp ground allspice
- 1 tsp ground cinnamon
- 3 tbsp sugar
- 1 egg, lightly beaten
- 3 tbsp olive oil
- 1 cup strong brewed coffee
- 3/4 cup raisins
- 1 1/2 tsp salt

Directions:

1. Add all ingredients except raisins to the bread maker pan.
2. Select the sweet bread cycle then select loaf size 1.5 pound and select crust color light. Press start.
3. Add raisins once add ingredient signal beeps.
4. Once done, remove the bread loaf from the bread maker.
5. Let cool bread loaf for 10 minutes.
6. Slice and serve.

Nutritional Value (Amount per Serving):

- Calories 191
- Fat 4.3 g
- Carbohydrates 34.6 g
- Sugar 8.5 g
- Protein 4.3 g
- Cholesterol 14 mg

Pumpkin Spice Bread

Preparation Time: 10 minutes
Cooking Time: 2 hours 50 minutes
Serve: 12

Ingredients:

- 2 eggs
- 1 1/2 tsp pumpkin pie spice
- 2 tsp baking powder
- 1 1/2 cups all-purpose flour
- 1 tsp vanilla
- 1/3 cup canola oil
- 1 cup pumpkin puree
- 1 cup white sugar
- 1/2 cup brown sugar
- 1/4 tsp salt

Directions:

1. Add all ingredients to the bread maker pan.
2. Select the sweet bread cycle then select loaf size 1.5 pound and select crust color medium. Press start.
3. Once done, remove the bread loaf from the bread maker.
4. Let cool bread loaf for 10 minutes.
5. Slice and serve.

Nutritional Value (Amount per Serving):

- Calories 216
- Fat 7 g
- Carbohydrates 36.8 g
- Sugar 23.4 g
- Protein 2.8 g
- Cholesterol 27 mg

Cardamom Cranberry Bread

Preparation Time: 10 minutes
Cooking Time: 2 hours 50 minutes
Serve: 12

Ingredients:

- 1 1/2 cups warm water
- 2 tbsp olive oil
- 4 cups flour
- 1 1/2 tsp cinnamon
- 1 1/2 tsp cardamom
- 1 cup dried cranberries
- 2 tsp yeast
- 2 tbsp brown sugar
- 1 1/2 tsp salt

Directions:

1. Add all ingredients except cranberries to the bread maker pan.
2. Select the sweet bread cycle then select loaf size 1.5 pound and select crust color light. Press start.
3. Add cranberries once add ingredient signal beeps.
4. Once done, remove the bread loaf from the bread maker.
5. Let cool bread loaf for 10 minutes.
6. Slice and serve.

Nutritional Value (Amount per Serving):

- Calories 186
- Fat 2.8 g
- Carbohydrates 34.8 g
- Sugar 1.9 g
- Protein 4.6 g
- Cholesterol 0 mg

Honey Oatmeal Sunflower Bread

Preparation Time: 10 minutes
Cooking Time: 2 hours 50 minutes
Serve: 12

Ingredients:

- 3 cups bread flour
- 1/2 cup old fashioned oats
- 2 tbsp milk powder
- 1 cup of water
- 1/4 cup honey
- 2 tbsp butter, softened
- 2 1/4 tsp active dry yeast
- 1/2 cup sunflower seeds
- 1 1/4 tsp salt

Directions:

1. Add all ingredients except sunflower seeds to the bread maker pan.
2. Select the sweet bread cycle then select loaf size 1.5 pound and select crust color medium. Press start.
3. Add sunflower seeds once add ingredient signal beeps.
4. Once done, remove the bread loaf from the bread maker.
5. Let cool bread loaf for 10 minutes.
6. Slice and serve.

Nutritional Value (Amount per Serving):

- Calories 197
- Fat 3.7 g
- Carbohydrates 35.5 g
- Sugar 6.8 g
- Protein 5.3 g
- Cholesterol 5 mg

Sweet Maple Bread

Preparation Time: 10 minutes
Cooking Time: 2 hours 50 minutes
Serve: 12

Ingredients:

- 2 cups bread flour
- 2 tsp bread machine yeast
- 1 cup cook oatmeal
- 1/3 cup maple syrup
- 1 tbsp olive oil
- 1 cup of water
- 1 tsp salt

Directions:

1. Add all ingredients to the bread maker pan.
2. Select the sweet bread cycle then select loaf size 1.5 pound and select crust color dark. Press start.
3. Once done, remove the bread loaf from the bread maker.
4. Let cool bread loaf for 10 minutes.
5. Slice and serve.

Nutritional Value (Amount per Serving):

- Calories 136
- Fat 1.9 g
- Carbohydrates 26.5 g
- Sugar 5.4 g
- Protein 3.3 g
- Cholesterol 0 mg

Chapter 8: Gluten-Free Bread

Moist Sandwich Bread

Preparation Time: 10 minutes
Cooking Time: 3 hours 32 minutes
Serve: 12

Ingredients:

- 4 eggs
- 4 tbsp butter
- 1 cup almond milk
- 1 1/4 tsp Xanthan gum
- 2 tsp instant yeast
- 3 tbsp sugar
- 3 cups gluten-free all-purpose flour
- 1 1/4 tsp salt

Directions:

1. Add all ingredients to the bread maker pan.
2. Select the gluten-free bread cycle then select loaf size 1.5 pound and select crust color medium. Press start.
3. Once done, remove the bread loaf from the bread maker.
4. Let cool bread loaf for 10 minutes.
5. Slice and serve.

Nutritional Value (Amount per Serving):

- Calories 221
- Fat 8.9 g
- Carbohydrates 31.3 g
- Sugar 6.9 g
- Protein 6.1 g
- Cholesterol 66 mg

Coconut Flour Bread

Preparation Time: 10 minutes
Cooking Time: 3 hours 32 minutes
Serve: 12

Ingredients:

- 4 eggs
- 2 tbsp honey
- 1/3 cup almond milk
- 1/2 cup olive oil
- 2 tsp baking powder
- 1/4 cup tapioca flour
- 1/3 cup ground flax meal
- 1/2 cup coconut flour
- 1/2 tsp sea salt

Directions:

1. Add all ingredients to the bread maker pan.
2. Select the gluten-free bread cycle then select loaf size 1.5 pound and select crust color medium. Press start.
3. Once done, remove the bread loaf from the bread maker.
4. Let cool bread loaf for 10 minutes.
5. Slice and serve.

Nutritional Value (Amount per Serving):

- Calories 167
- Fat 13.7 g
- Carbohydrates 9.8 g
- Sugar 4.2 g
- Protein 3.7 g
- Cholesterol 55 mg

Whole-Grain Bread

Preparation Time: 10 minutes
Cooking Time: 3 hours 32 minutes
Serve: 12

Ingredients:

- 3 eggs
- 2 1/4 tsp active dry yeast
- 3 tbsp non-dairy creamer
- 3 tbsp sugar
- 4 1/2 tsp Xanthan gum
- 1/2 cup garbanzo bean flour
- 1/2 cup potato starch
- 1/2 cup tapioca flour
- 2 cups brown rice flour
- 1/4 cup canola oil
- 1 tsp apple cider vinegar
- 1 1/2 cusp hot water
- 1 1/2 tsp sea salt

Directions:

1. Add all ingredients to the bread maker pan.
2. Select the gluten-free bread cycle then select loaf size 1.5 pound and select crust color medium. Press start.
3. Once done, remove the bread loaf from the bread maker.
4. Let cool bread loaf for 10 minutes.
5. Slice and serve.

Nutritional Value (Amount per Serving):

- Calories 229
- Fat 7.3 g
- Carbohydrates 37 g
- Sugar 3.3 g
- Protein 4.7 g
- Cholesterol 41 mg

Gluten-Free Flour Bread

Preparation Time: 10 minutes
Cooking Time: 3 hours 32 minutes
Serve: 12

Ingredients:

- 3 eggs
- 1 tbsp yeast
- 17 oz Gluten-free flour
- 1 tbsp sugar
- 4 oz almond milk
- 8 oz water
- 1 tsp apple cider vinegar
- 1 1/2 tbsp olive oil
- 1 tsp salt

Directions:

1. Add all ingredients to the bread maker pan.
2. Select the gluten-free bread cycle then select loaf size 1.5 pound and select crust color medium. Press start.
3. Once done, remove the bread loaf from the bread maker.
4. Let cool bread loaf for 10 minutes.
5. Slice and serve.

Nutritional Value (Amount per Serving):

- Calories 203
- Fat 5.7 g
- Carbohydrates 34.1 g
- Sugar 2.4 g
- Protein 4.4 g
- Cholesterol 41 mg

Sandwich Bread

Preparation Time: 10 minutes
Cooking Time: 3 hours 32 minutes
Serve: 12

Ingredients:

- 3 cups gluten-free all-purpose baking flour
- 2 tsp active dry yeast
- 1 tbsp potato flour
- 3/4 tsp plain soy
- 1 tsp guar gum
- 1 tbsp Xanthan gum
- 2 tbsp sugar
- 1 tsp lemon juice
- 1/4 cup olive oil
- 3/4 cup whole egg
- 1 1/2 cups warm soy milk
- 3/4 tsp sea salt

Directions:

1. Add all ingredients to the bread maker pan.
2. Select the gluten-free bread cycle then select loaf size 1.5 pound and select crust color medium. Press start.
3. Once done, remove the bread loaf from the bread maker.
4. Let cool bread loaf for 10 minutes.
5. Slice and serve.

Nutritional Value (Amount per Serving):

- Calories 194
- Fat 6.8 g
- Carbohydrates 28.1 g
- Sugar 3.4 g
- Protein 6.3 g
- Cholesterol 57 mg

Gluten-Free Cinnamon Raisin Bread

Preparation Time: 10 minutes
Cooking Time: 3 hours 32 minutes
Serve: 12

Ingredients:

- 3 eggs
- 1/2 cup raisins
- 3 tsp cinnamon
- 3 tbsp sugar
- 3 tsp psyllium husk
- 1/4 cup flaxseed meal
- 1/3 cup tapioca flour
- 2/3 cup potato starch
- 2 cups white rice flour
- 2 1/4 tsp bread machine yeast
- 2 tbsp honey
- 1 tsp apple cider vinegar
- 3 tbsp olive oil
- 2/3 cup almond milk
- 1 cup of water
- 1 1/2 tsp salt

Directions:

1. Add all ingredients except raisins to the bread maker pan in the listed order.
2. Select the gluten-free bread cycle then select loaf size 1.5 pound and select crust color medium. Press start.
3. Add raisins once add ingredient signal beeps.
4. Once done, remove the bread loaf from the bread maker.
5. Let cool bread loaf for 10 minutes.
6. Slice and serve.

Nutritional Value (Amount per Serving):

- Calories 267
- Fat 8.9 g

- Carbohydrates 44.3 g
- Sugar 10.1 g
- Protein 4.2 g
- Cholesterol 41 mg

Gluten-Free Bread

Preparation Time: 10 minutes
Cooking Time: 3 hours 32 minutes
Serve: 12

Ingredients:

- 2 eggs
- 1 3/4 cup warm water
- 1 tsp vinegar
- 1/4 cup olive oil
- 1 packet dry yeast
- 3 1/2 tsp Xanthan gum
- 1/4 cup sugar
- 1 1/3 cup powdered milk
- 2 cups white rice flour
- 1 cup brown rice flour
- 1 1/2 tsp salt

Directions:

1. Add all ingredients to the bread maker pan.
2. Select the gluten-free bread cycle then select loaf size 1.5 pound and select crust color medium. Press start.
3. Once done, remove the bread loaf from the bread maker.
4. Let cool bread loaf for 10 minutes.
5. Slice and serve.

Nutritional Value (Amount per Serving):

- Calories 263
- Fat 5.7 g
- Carbohydrates 45 g
- Sugar 11.5 g
- Protein 9.1 g
- Cholesterol 30 mg

Gluten-Free Banana Bread

Preparation Time: 10 minutes
Cooking Time: 3 hours 32 minutes
Serve: 12

Ingredients:

- 2 eggs
- 2 cups gluten-free baking flour
- 1 tsp baking soda
- 1 tsp ground cinnamon
- 4 ripe bananas, mashed
- 1 tbsp vanilla
- 1/4 cup brown sugar
- 1/4 cup sugar
- 1/2 cup butter, melted
- 1/2 tsp salt

Directions:

1. Add all ingredients to the bread maker pan.
2. Select the gluten-free bread cycle then select loaf size 1.5 pound and select crust color medium. Press start.
3. Once done, remove the bread loaf from the bread maker.
4. Let cool bread loaf for 10 minutes.
5. Slice and serve.

Nutritional Value (Amount per Serving):

- Calories 214
- Fat 8.9 g
- Carbohydrates 31.1 g
- Sugar 12.1 g
- Protein 3.4 g
- Cholesterol 48 mg

Gluten-Free French Bread

Preparation Time: 10 minutes
Cooking Time: 3 hours 32 minutes
Serve: 12

Ingredients:

- 1 tbsp butter
- 1 tsp apple cider vinegar
- 1 tbsp honey
- 1 egg white
- 6 oz warm water
- 2 tsp instant yeast
- 1/4 cup tapioca starch
- 3/4 tsp Xanthan gum
- 1 3/4 cups gluten-free all-purpose flour
- 1/2 tsp kosher salt

Directions:

1. Add all ingredients to the bread maker pan.
2. Select the gluten-free bread cycle then select loaf size 1.5 pound and select crust color medium. Press start.
3. Once done, remove the bread loaf from the bread maker.
4. Let cool bread loaf for 10 minutes.
5. Slice and serve.

Nutritional Value (Amount per Serving):

- Calories 91
- Fat 1.3 g
- Carbohydrates 19.4 g
- Sugar 1.6 g
- Protein 2.5 g
- Cholesterol 3 mg

Multiseed Multigrain Sandwich Bread

Preparation Time: 10 minutes
Cooking Time: 3 hours 32 minutes
Serve: 12

Ingredients:

- 3 eggs
- 3 tbsp molasses
- 1 tsp apple cider vinegar
- 3 tbsp olive oil
- 1 cup of warm water
- 4 1/2 tsp active dry yeast
- 1 tbsp Xanthan gum
- 1 tbsp cocoa powder
- 1 cup tapioca starch
- 1/2 cup brown rice flour
- 1/2 cup millet flour
- 1 cup sorghum flour
- 1/2 cup milk powder
- 1 1/2 tsp salt

Directions:

1. Add all ingredients to the bread maker pan.
2. Select the gluten-free bread cycle then select loaf size 1.5 pound and select crust color medium. Press start.
3. Once done, remove the bread loaf from the bread maker.
4. Let cool bread loaf for 10 minutes.
5. Slice and serve.

Nutritional Value (Amount per Serving):

- Calories 219
- Fat 5.5 g
- Carbohydrates 37.5 g
- Sugar 6 g
- Protein 6.6 g
- Cholesterol 42 mg

Chapter 9: Sourdough Bread

Healthy Sourdough Bread

Preparation Time: 10 minutes
Cooking Time: 2 hours 53 minutes
Serve: 12

Ingredients:

- 12 oz sourdough starter
- 3 tbsp sucanat
- 4 cups bread flour
- 6 oz warm water
- 1 3/4 tsp sea salt

Directions:

1. In a bowl, mix half bread flour, starter, and water. Cover and let the mixture stand for overnight.
2. Add remaining ingredients into the mixture and mix until well combined.
3. Add bread mixture to the bread maker pan.
4. Select the basic bread cycle then select loaf size 1.5 pound and select crust color light. Press start.
5. Once done, remove the bread loaf from the bread maker.
6. Let cool bread loaf for 10 minutes.
7. Slice and serve.

Nutritional Value (Amount per Serving):

- Calories 233
- Fat 1.2 g
- Carbohydrates 48 g
- Sugar 3.5 g
- Protein 6.8 g
- Cholesterol 0 mg

Jalapeno Cheddar Sourdough Bread

Preparation Time: 10 minutes
Cooking Time: 2 hours 53 minutes
Serve: 12

Ingredients:

- 1/4 cup sourdough starter
- 1/4 cup chives, minced
- 1 cup cheddar cheese, shredded
- 1/3 cup pickled jalapenos, sliced
- 1/4 cup whole wheat flour
- 1 3/4 cups all-purpose flour
- 2 1/3 cups bread flour
- 1 1/2 cup warm water
- 1 1/2 tsp sea salt

Directions:

1. In a bowl, mix half bread flour, starter, and water. Cover and let the mixture stand for overnight.
2. Add remaining ingredients into the mixture and mix until well combined.
3. Add bread mixture to the bread maker pan.
4. Select the basic bread cycle then select loaf size 1.5 pound and select crust color light. Press start.
5. Once done, remove the bread loaf from the bread maker.
6. Let cool bread loaf for 10 minutes.
7. Slice and serve.

Nutritional Value (Amount per Serving):

- Calories 206
- Fat 3.7 g
- Carbohydrates 35.2 g
- Sugar 0.2 g
- Protein 7.1 g
- Cholesterol 10 mg

Sourdough Rye Bread

Preparation Time: 10 minutes
Cooking Time: 2 hours 53 minutes
Serve: 12

Ingredients:

- 1 egg white
- 2 tbsp caraway seeds
- 2 tsp table salt
- 1 tbsp malt syrup
- 2 1/2 cups bread flour
- 1 cup ground rye flour
- 1 1/2 cups warm water
- 1 cup active sourdough starter

Directions:

1. In a bowl, mix half bread flour, starter, and water. Cover and let the mixture stand for overnight.
2. Add remaining ingredients into the mixture and mix until well combined.
3. Add bread mixture to the bread maker pan.
4. Select the basic bread cycle then select loaf size 1.5 pound and select crust color light. Press start.
5. Once done, remove the bread loaf from the bread maker.
6. Let cool bread loaf for 10 minutes.
7. Slice and serve.

Nutritional Value (Amount per Serving):

- Calories 153
- Fat 0.6 g
- Carbohydrates 31.7 g
- Sugar 1.8 g
- Protein 4.7 g
- Cholesterol 0 mg

Soft Whole Wheat Sourdough Bread

Preparation Time: 10 minutes
Cooking Time: 2 hours 53 minutes
Serve: 12

Ingredients:

- 2/3 cup warm water
- 2 tsp butter, melted
- 1 1/2 cups all-purpose flour
- 1 cup sourdough starter
- 3/4 tsp dry active yeast
- 1 cup whole wheat flour
- 1 1/2 tsp salt

Directions:

1. In a bowl, mix half whole wheat flour, starter, and water. Cover and let the mixture stand for overnight.
2. Add remaining ingredients into the mixture and mix until well combined.
3. Add bread mixture to the bread maker pan.
4. Select the basic bread cycle then select loaf size 1.5 pound and select crust color light. Press start.
5. Once done, remove the bread loaf from the bread maker.
6. Let cool bread loaf for 10 minutes.
7. Slice and serve.

Nutritional Value (Amount per Serving):

- Calories 113
- Fat 1 g
- Carbohydrates 22.2 g
- Sugar 0.2 g
- Protein 3.2 g
- Cholesterol 2 mg

Whole Wheat Sandwich Bread

Preparation Time: 10 minutes
Cooking Time: 2 hours 53 minutes
Serve: 12

Ingredients:

- 2/3 cup warm water
- 1 tsp butter, melted
- 1 1/2 cups all-purpose flour
- 1 cup whole wheat flour
- 1 cup sourdough starter
- 3/4 tsp dry active yeast
- 1 1/2 tsp salt

Directions:

1. In a bowl, mix half flour, starter, and water. Cover and let the mixture stand for overnight.
2. Add remaining ingredients into the mixture and mix until well combined.
3. Add bread mixture to the bread maker pan.
4. Select the basic bread cycle then select loaf size 1.5 pound and select crust color light. Press start.
5. Once done, remove the bread loaf from the bread maker.
6. Let cool bread loaf for 10 minutes.
7. Slice and serve.

Nutritional Value (Amount per Serving):

- Calories 110
- Fat 0.7 g
- Carbohydrates 22.2 g
- Sugar 0.2 g
- Protein 3.2 g
- Cholesterol 1 mg

Simple Sourdough Bread

Preparation Time: 10 minutes
Cooking Time: 2 hours 53 minutes
Serve: 12

Ingredients:

- 3 cups bread flour
- 1/2 tsp sugar
- 3/4 cup sourdough starter
- 1 cup of warm water
- 1 3/4 tsp salt

Directions:

1. In a bowl, mix half bread flour, starter, and water. Cover and let the mixture stand for overnight.
2. Add remaining ingredients into the mixture and mix until well combined.
3. Add bread mixture to the bread maker pan.
4. Select the basic bread cycle then select loaf size 1.5 pound and select crust color light. Press start.
5. Once done, remove the bread loaf from the bread maker.
6. Let cool bread loaf for 10 minutes.
7. Slice and serve.

Nutritional Value (Amount per Serving):

- Calories 123
- Fat 0.4 g
- Carbohydrates 25.7 g
- Sugar 0.4 g
- Protein 3.5 g
- Cholesterol 0 mg

Basic Sourdough Bread

Preparation Time: 10 minutes
Cooking Time: 2 hours 53 minutes
Serve: 12

Ingredients:

- 1 1/4 cups sourdough starter
- 2 tsp bread machine yeast
- 1 tbsp sugar
- 3 cups bread flour
- 1 tbsp butter
- 1/3 cup water
- 1 tsp salt

Directions:

1. In a bowl, mix half flour, starter, and water. Cover and let the mixture stand for overnight.
2. Add remaining ingredients into the mixture and mix until well combined.
3. Add bread mixture to the bread maker pan.
4. Select the basic bread cycle then select loaf size 1.5 pound and select crust color light. Press start.
5. Once done, remove the bread loaf from the bread maker.
6. Let cool bread loaf for 10 minutes.
7. Slice and serve.

Nutritional Value (Amount per Serving):

- Calories 143
- Fat 1.5 g
- Carbohydrates 27.9 g
- Sugar 1.3 g
- Protein 4 g
- Cholesterol 3 mg

Maple Oat Sourdough Bread

Preparation Time: 10 minutes
Cooking Time: 2 hours 53 minutes
Serve: 12

Ingredients:

- 1 cup rolled oats, soak for 30 minutes
- 2 1/4 cups bread flour
- 1/2 cup whole wheat bread flour
- 1 tbsp olive oil
- 1/4 cup maple syrup
- 1 cup of warm water
- 3/4 cup sourdough starter
- 1 1/2 tsp sea salt

Directions:

1. In a bowl, mix half bread flour, starter, and water. Cover and let the mixture stand for overnight.
2. Add remaining ingredients into the mixture and mix until well combined.
3. Add bread mixture to the bread maker pan.
4. Select the basic bread cycle then select loaf size 1.5 pound and select crust color light. Press start.
5. Once done, remove the bread loaf from the bread maker.
6. Let cool bread loaf for 10 minutes.
7. Slice and serve.

Nutritional Value (Amount per Serving):

- Calories 168
- Fat 2 g
- Carbohydrates 33.3 g
- Sugar 4.2 g
- Protein 4.5 g
- Cholesterol 0 mg

Gluten-Free Bread

Preparation Time: 10 minutes
Cooking Time: 2 hours 53 minutes
Serve: 12

Ingredients:

- 1 cup gluten-free sourdough starter
- 1 tbsp pink salt
- 1 tbsp maple syrup
- 2/3 cup ground flax seeds
- 1 cup of water
- 1 cup gluten-free oat flour
- 1 cup buckwheat flour
- 1/2 cup brown rice flour

Directions:

1. In a bowl, mix half oat flour, starter, and water. Cover and let the mixture stand for overnight.
2. Add remaining ingredients into the mixture and mix until well combined.
3. Add bread mixture to the bread maker pan.
4. Select the basic bread cycle then select loaf size 1.5 pound and select crust color light. Press start.
5. Once done, remove the bread loaf from the bread maker.
6. Let cool bread loaf for 10 minutes.
7. Slice and serve.

Nutritional Value (Amount per Serving):

- Calories 127
- Fat 2.8 g
- Carbohydrates 20.8 g
- Sugar 1.6 g
- Protein 4.2 g
- Cholesterol 0 mg

Easy Sourdough Bread

Preparation Time: 10 minutes
Cooking Time: 2 hours 53 minutes
Serve: 12

Ingredients:

- 1 cup sourdough starter
- 3 tbsp olive oil
- 3 cups bread flour
- 1 tbsp active dry yeast
- 1 tbsp sugar
- 3/4 cup warm water
- 2 tsp salt

Directions:

1. In a bowl, mix half bread flour, starter, and water. Cover and let the mixture stand for overnight.
2. Add remaining ingredients into the mixture and mix until well combined.
3. Add bread mixture to the bread maker pan.
4. Select the basic bread cycle then select loaf size 1.5 pound and select crust color light. Press start.
5. Once done, remove the bread loaf from the bread maker.
6. Let cool bread loaf for 10 minutes.
7. Slice and serve.

Nutritional Value (Amount per Serving):

- Calories 162
- Fat 4 g
- Carbohydrates 27.5 g
- Sugar 1.3 g
- Protein 4 g
- Cholesterol 0 mg

Conclusion

The Mediterranean lifestyle encourages physical exercise and enjoying the meals you make with friends and family. Even if you just bought a Mediterranean bread machine, this book will be your guide through everything you need to know. That means you will get access to some of the top-chef recipes for making the perfect bread from all around Mediterranean.

Switch to a new diet making a lifestyle change can be tough! This book will help you step-by-step to afford this journey and will prepare you to understand this Mediterranean

lifestyle and finally benefit from it lifelong. The Mediterranean Bread Machine Cookbook for Beginners will let you become a master baker in a matter of hours with the information and advice inside!

www.ingramcontent.com/pod-product-compliance
Lightning Source LLC
Chambersburg PA
CBHW081402070526
44583CB00020B/2644